To Mum,
Hoping this will bring
back happy me
Lots of love
Neville & Lu

G000129119

PEMBROKE DOCK

Pembroke Dock
The Town Built to Build Ships

By Phil Carradice

Published by Accent Press Ltd – 2006

www.accentpress.co.uk

ISBN 1-905170-18-1 / 978-1-905170-18-0

Printed and bound in the UK
Typeset by Carnegie Book Production

Contents

Foreword

PEMBROKE DOCK HAS BEEN in existence for less than two hundred years, but in that time it has seen the heights of success and the depths of failure. It has seen human tragedy, pomp and circumstance, royal visitors and even the wiping away of the shipbuilding industry that brought the town into existence. As if that were not enough, a series of bombing raids during World War Two nearly obliterated the town.

There is an old cliché that says, 'You can take the boy out of Pembroke Dock, but you can never take Pembroke Dock out of the boy.' I suppose you can change the town in that line to fit whichever community you like, but with Pembroke Dock it is particularly appropriate. You might well leave the town, move on to other places, other experiences, but the town will never leave you.

Like me, Phil Carradice comes from a family that has deep-rooted connections to the place. And in *The Town Built to Build Ships* he has produced a book that is full of engaging stories, full of real character. This is not just a local history; it is the story of a community, detailing how that community fits in with the larger scheme of things. It makes fascinating reading, catching the feel of the town and its people but, at the same time, placing it in its historical and sociological context. It is a book to be read and enjoyed.

After you have read it – go and see Pembroke Dock for yourself. Even if you have lived there for fifty years, look at it again, look at it with different eyes. You will not be disappointed.

Jamie Owen, Cardiff,
August 2006

Introduction

O VER THE PAST TWENTY or thirty years the town of Pembroke Dock has seen more visitors than at any time in its, admittedly, brief history. Interestingly, that huge influx of visitors has been almost totally due to the same elements that brought the town into existence in the first place – the sea and ships.

The recent developments and gradual increase in people passing through the town have been largely due to the Irish ferry service, now based in the eastern part of the old dockyard. The original purpose behind the place was, quite simply, to build ships, warships for the Royal Navy.

Most present-day visitors to the town, even those ferry passengers who regularly and happily trundle through the streets and, eventually, through the walls of the old dockyard with their minds focused on holidays or jobs ahead, have little or no understanding of what they are passing.

It is understandable. Little has been written about the town and dock-yard at Pembroke Dock. The place has been largely forgotten and, these days, warrants little more than a casual mention in most naval histories. Visitors might be excused for thinking that the remains of buildings and walls, so casually glimpsed through car or lorry windows as they speed into the ferry port, hold little more than a few minor slipways and jetties. How wrong they are.

Interminable building work, the stark outlines of the ferry terminal and jetty, the numerous local business initiatives that have come and gone with increasing regularity over the years, may well dominate the remains of the dockyard these days. They tell nothing of the glory and the fame that were once inextricably linked to the name of Pembroke Dock.

The Royal Naval Dockyard at Pembroke Dock was the only such establishment to exist in Wales – if you discount the short lived and misguided venture at nearby Milford. Founded in 1814, for a brief span of 112 years the yard at Pembroke Dock was one of the most important shipbuilding centres in the country, arguably the world. The Chief

Constructor of the US Navy once apparently called the place 'the first shipbuilding yards in the world'. The man in question was Philip Hichborn and what he actually said was that while the yards were wonderful for building they had just one dock and no basins and, therefore, their scope was limited. Despite this undoubtedly accurate appraisal and assessment of Pembroke Dock's limitations – limitations that prevented the yards from quite making it to the top grade of British dockyards – the place was renowned for the quality of its workmanship and for the sleek lines of the ships that it built.

From even the most casual of investigations it is clear that the warships built at Pembroke Dock were the envy of other yards. They were, for a brief and glorious period, so innovative and revolutionary that they changed the whole nature and design of shipbuilding. It can also be argued that they changed the course of naval history.

The town of Pembroke Dock followed quickly and easily on the heels of the dockyard. In all respects a 'new town' of the nineteenth century, the town was mapped out on a grid-like pattern with wide streets and an elegance that speaks of self-importance and a clear plan for the future. It is as if the place was waiting for prosperity – prosperity that did not come. Unlike most British towns it did not grow and evolve over the years. Pembroke Dock literally burst into existence in the years after 1814 – it remains a social historian's dream, a community with a precise and exact moment of creation.

It is still possible to gain a flavour of the old dockyard, provided you have at least a degree of imagination and are prepared to venture beyond the main thoroughfares of the town. Walk out along the beach at Front Street when the tide is low or, perhaps, stand on the great bulk of Hobbs Point jetty. Gaze back at the remains of the once proud yards. Half close the eyes and imagine the great warships, the *Renown* and *Duke of Wellington*, the *Hannibal*, *Drake* and *Repulse*, sliding easily down the launching ways. The names and the images are evocative beyond belief. There is no doubt that this was once a very special place.

The dockyard may be gone but the memories remain. Perhaps the star of Pembroke Dock burned too quickly and too brightly to survive for long, rather like the moth that flickers too close, too fervently, towards the dancing flame. A period of just over one hundred years is not long for a venture like a Royal Dockyard to exist and when the yards closed in 1926 the town that had been created solely to build ships was suddenly left without reason for existence.

Despite dozens of attempts to breathe life back into this quiet, stranded community at the farthest corner of west Wales the years since 1926 have been largely unproductive and depressing. These days the town has only its history and its memories to cling to. But what memories they are!

CHAPTER ONE

Before the Town Began

THE MODERN TOWN OF Pembroke Dock stands on a flat, sheltered shelf of land on the southern shore of the Cleddau River, close to that rather ill-defined or unclear spot where the river ends and the broad expanse of Milford Haven begins. Approximately nine miles from the sea, Pembroke Dock nestles easily between the Cleddau to the north and a sharply rising ridge to the south. Beyond the ridge lie the muddy but dangerously tidal Pembroke River and the ancient town and castle of Pembroke itself. Beyond that again is the wild expanse of the South Pembrokeshire peninsula.

The town of Pembroke Dock did not exist until 1814 but the influence of man had long been felt in the area. South Pembrokeshire is dominated by the sunken valley of Milford Haven and this, combined with the region's long golden beaches, meant that travellers and settlers alike had always been attracted here.

Evidence of man's first settlement in Pembrokeshire can be found in several of the caves that nestle into the carboniferous limestone outcrops in the south of the county. The hunting people of the Palaeolithic, Mesolithic and Neolithic periods were amongst the first arrivals in the area, making their homes in caves like the one to be found at Priory Farm Cave, Catshole Quarry, just down river from the town of Pembroke. These early people lived close to the entrance of such caves — after all, the dark was always something to be feared and the simple process of lighting fires near the entrances would help to keep away wild animals. These early people lived off the land, hunting and fishing, and littered the floors of their caves with bones, the remains of food and stone implements.

Animals such as mammoth, reindeer and horse were roaming the country at the time — ideal hunting fodder for early man. The first evidence of human habitation in Pembrokeshire can be found in the shape of Palaeolithic man, who relied on these creatures for his food supplies, and dates to about 10,000 BC. This was towards the end of the Ice Age when the climate was gradually changing from cold, dry conditions to what W. F. Grimes has called 'the warmer and wetter version of the climate of today.'

In due course, the Palaeolithic age was followed by the Mesolithic. The Mesolithic people were hunters and fishers who had learned the skill of stone chipping and so produced far more sophisticated blades and weapons than their predecessors. They were, in their turn, succeeded by Neolithic man, who arrived in numbers, probably by sea, sailing up the Haven in simple skin boats that were not dissimilar to modern Welsh coracles. They brought with them a real knowledge of agriculture, albeit primitive and unsophisticated by our standards. They began to cultivate the land and the face of Pembrokeshire, as we know it, was already starting to be formed.

The rural nature of the area soon to be known as Pembroke Dock can be seen in this early view.

These Neolithic people were the builders of the great stone cromlechs that still litter the county of Pembrokeshire. While the north of the county is, perhaps, more lavishly endowed with examples of such burial chambers and standing stones, there are several prehistoric sites of note in the

south. Of particular importance are the chambers at Angle, Manorbier and Burton on the northern shore of the Cleddau River.

Bronze Age settlers, Beaker Folk as they were called, came next although, obviously, there were long periods when Bronze Age and Neolithic people existed almost side by side and inter-marriage was reasonably common. Bronze Age people closely resembled modern man, having rounded heads – in contrast to the distinctive elongated heads of the Neolithic folk. The Iron Age gradually replaced the Bronze Age when the Celtic immigrants, from what is now Germany and France, began to journey to Pembrokeshire. They came because of the growth of sea trading and spoke a language a little similar to modern Welsh.

By the time the Romans arrived in Britain the Celtic tribe living in Pembrokeshire were the Demetae. For many years historians believed that the Roman occupation barely touched this remote corner of west Wales. Admittedly, there have been few archaeological discoveries from the period but it remains a strange, not to say naive, assumption. While the Romans may not have been here in huge numbers it would be foolish to imagine that such an adventurous and acquisitive people did not venture

Idyllic rural Pembrokeshire – who would have suspected what was to come?

bravely up the broad waters of the Haven at some stage in their occupation of these islands.

Part of the problem comes from the fact that no Roman forts have been discovered in Pembrokeshire. The Demetae apparently co-operated with the Romans, mainly because the invaders had defeated the Silures, traditional enemies of the Demetae. Therefore the popularly held belief is that the Romans were happy to use the Demetae as controllers or guardians of the area and so had little or no need to build forts. There is more than a grain of truth in the theory but recently discovered Auxiliary forts in the Carmarthenshire area have called the belief into question.

The closest known Roman fort to Pembrokeshire was at Carmarthen itself, Maridunum as it was called, and there were also small (and possibly temporary) establishments at Castle Flemish and at Cwmbryn. Two large forts have recently been unearthed just outside Llandeilo but these have not yet been fully excavated. Militarily, however, this seems to have been the limit of Roman involvement, although recent archaeological surveys do seem to indicate that the Romans did actually build a road into Pembrokeshire, reaching at least as far as the Wiston area.

Where the Roman incursion went after Wiston remains unclear. Whether the road snaked north towards present day Fishguard or curved south to Milford Haven is a matter of debate. Until there is further clear evidence, historians can only make educated guesses.

To make matters a little more clouded, coins dating from the reign of Claudius Gothicus (AD 268–270) and Constantius (AD 337–361) have been found at Pennar, to the south of Pembroke Dock, and on the site of Pembroke Castle. Whether these coins were deposited in the area at the time of the Roman occupation or taken and left there at a later date remains unknown.

However, a Roman fleet was permanently based at what is now the city of Cardiff and patrolled the Bristol Channel area as a defence against raiders from Ireland who made repeated attacks on the Pembrokeshire coast from about AD 290. It would have been logical for such a fleet to make use of Milford Haven, one of the finest natural harbours in the world. Possibly, then, this is the source of the coins found in the Pembroke and Pembroke Dock area. The Irish attacks were finally ended at the close of the fourth century and the Roman fleet, like all the occupying forces, already under pressure to return to Rome, would have come no more.

A Roman villa has recently been discovered in the northern part of the county, although whether this was the home of a retired soldier or a Romano-British chieftain has yet to be confirmed. Apart from the recently discovered track to Wiston, there were few Roman roads in this part of Wales, even though roads were built between Carmarthen and Brecon and northwards from Carmarthen towards the present-day town of Aberystwyth.

So the situation regarding Roman involvement remains somewhat unclear. What is known is that with the collapse of the Roman Empire, their capital sacked in AD 410, the period referred to – perhaps a little unfairly – as the Dark Ages descended across the land. In the fourth century the Deisi from the Irish area around Waterford settled in the county, establishing a dynasty that lasted for several hundred years – it was to be a troubled and troublesome period.

From earliest times the sea around Pembrokeshire had been important. Early Christian missionaries now used it as a means of travelling into Britain and avoiding the raiding Norsemen. Local legend declares that St Patrick, the patron saint of Ireland, came to Pembrokeshire and considered creating a church or shrine on the spot where St David's Cathedral was later built. However, a vision told him that this place was reserved for another man, St David himself, who would arrive thirty years later. St Patrick left for Ireland and immortality.

There are dozens of legends about the Celtic saints, not least St Govan whose tiny church nestles into the cliffs below St Govan's Head. Fifty-two steps lead down to the church – they are never the same when you count them on the climb back up! Legend states that St Govan hid here when menaced by Viking raiders. The rocks closed in around his body to keep him safe.

Viking marauders raided the Pembrokeshire coast many times, particularly between AD 844 and 1091. The cathedral of St David's was burned on eight separate occasions, despite its location in a deep hollow that was, and is, invisible from the sea. In all probability the raiders used the safe anchorage of Milford Haven as a temporary base many times during the Roman with-drawal and the establishment of the Deisi as the ruling tribe in the area.

The Viking chieftain Huba almost certainly gave his name to Hubberston, a small village at the mouth of the estuary, after he wintered there in AD 877. He apparently had with him a fleet of 23 ships and 2,000 warriors. The effect on the local birth rate can only be imagined!

Carr Rocks off the town of Pembroke Dock – so called on all the earliest charts of the Haven – derive their name from the Norse word 'skare', which means rocks. The flat land to the east of Carr Rocks, the site of the later dockyard, would have been an ideal sheltering spot for any visiting Norseman. It is conjecture but highly likely that the area was visited by the Vikings on many occasions.

There are over twenty place names in Pembrokeshire that have a Norse derivation – Skokholm and Skomer islands and the town of Goodwick being only a few. The famous Olaf Haroldston spent several months in the county in 1091 and by 1100 there were a large number of Viking settlements, proving that the Norsemen did not only come to ravage and take plunder. Sometimes they came to settle and make a home.

However, it was the arrival of the Normans – themselves descended from the Norse peoples – at the end of the eleventh century that brought significant and definitive change. Pembroke Castle was established by Arnulph de Montgomery in 1093, twenty-seven years after the victory of Duke William at the Battle of Hastings. During this interim period it was very much a 'hands off' affair as far as Wales was concerned. William did actually make a pilgrimage to the cathedral at St David's several years into his reign – there are even those who claim it was a spying mission, prior to a future invasion, but this is highly unlikely, not to say impossible, when you consider the eventual style of Norman incursion into Wales.

An agreement between William and Rhys ap Tewdwr, King of Deheubarth – which at that time, included the Pembrokeshire area – stated that Rhys would retain authority over his kingdom, provided he did not make any incursions across Offa's Dyke. It was an arrangement that gave Wales a small breathing space. However, when Rhys was killed in battle in 1093 the Norman Barons were quick to make their move.

The Norman conquest of Wales was a piecemeal affair, conducted by the great Marcher Lords, the Earls of Hereford, Shrewsbury and Chester, not by the King who was content to let his turbulent Barons conquer and control a potentially dangerous part of his kingdom.

Roger de Montgomery, Earl of Shrewsbury, began his assault over the mountains of mid Wales barely one week after the death of Rhys ap Tewdwr and by the beginning of July 1093 his forces had overrun Ceridigion, the northern part of the Kingdom of Deheubarth. He built the castle of Cardigan but it was clear that his real aim was the rich land of the south, the area now known as Pembrokeshire.

Roger's son, Arnulph, probably arrived at Pembroke by boat, sailing up the Haven in what was actually something of a commando raid. Almost immediately he realised the potential of the headland at Pembroke as a site for a castle. He built what Giraldus Cambrensis later described as 'a slender

PBK 66   PEMBROKE, VIEW FROM THE CASTLE.   Copyright Frith's

fortress of stakes and turf' and over the next few decades the area became
the major base for Norman activities in west Wales.

A series of castles, originally motte and baileys but soon replaced by strong
stone fortifications, was strung across the neck of the south Pembrokeshire
peninsula, effectively creating a buffer between the Normans (and the
Flemish wool merchants brought into the area to trade and work) and the
warlike Welsh to the north and east. Known as the Landsker, this psycho-
logical barrier – ominously bolstered by castles like Carew, Roch and
Llawhaden – helped create two separate types of people within one county.
To the north lived those who spoke Welsh and to the south, clustered
primarily around the towns and fortresses of Pembroke, Haverfordwest
and Tenby, were those who spoke English.

The Earldom and County Palatine of Pembroke were created in 1138
although the town of Pembroke did not receive a Charter of Incorporation
until the reign of King Richard III. Despite this, the town gradually grew
in size and importance, as did the surrounding countryside. Writing in
1595 the historian George Owen drew attention to the oyster beds at
nearby Pennar:

> Pennar Mouth is the creeke that cometh up to Pembroke town, this
> being the largest creeke in all Milford. It passeth up into the land

Pembroke Castle,
besieged and battered
over the centuries,
was the main power
base for the Normans
and, until the
coming of Pembroke
Dockyard, the most
significant military
establishment in
south-west Wales.

three myles. The Crowe is a hollow or shelf a pretty way within the entrance of Pennar Mouth and it is an oyster bed and on the Crowe groweth one of the best Oysters of all Milford being a big and sweet oyster. The poor people thereabouts are greatly relieved by the oysters for upon lowe water the bed is drie and the people gather the oysters there without any dredge or other helpe of boate.

Milford Haven remained an important strategic centre throughout the Middle Ages. Richard Strongbow, son of the first Earl of Pembroke, Gilbert de Clare, used Pembroke Castle as his base during the systematic and brutal conquest of Ireland. In 1172 Henry II gathered together a fleet of over 400 ships, the largest gathering of vessels to assemble in Milford Haven, for the assault. In 1397 Richard II also left for Ireland from the Haven.

Owain Glyndwr and a band of French mercenaries landed in the Haven in an abortive raid in 1405 while the area also provided the more successful landing site for Henry Tudor's return from exile in 1485. The first Tudor king had been born in Pembroke Castle in 1457 and, somehow, it seems fitting that his victorious march to defeat Richard at Bosworth Field should have begun almost within sighting distance of his birthplace.

By the end of the seventeenth century, despite the severe privations of the Civil War when the town was bombarded and besieged by no less a person than Oliver Cromwell, Pembroke was an important centre of trade. With over 200 vessels registered to the port it was probably the richest community in the whole of south Wales.

As far as the future town of Pembroke Dock was concerned, the land on which it now stands had been claimed by the Normans when Arnulph de Montgomery landed in 1093. A tower, which still stands within the dock-

Paterchurch Tower and the ruins of the old mansion. This drawing by Adams dates from the end of the eighteenth century when nothing but these stones and a few isolated farms disturbed the sweep of the land.

yard walls, is the sole remnant of the period. Known as Patrickchurch or Paterchurch Tower, the building gave its name to the immediate area but its origins remain clouded in mystery. There are those who believe it was a watch-tower for nearby Pembroke Castle although its position to the north of the ridge separating it from Pembroke, shielded by trees and dense vegetation, means that it has always been invisible from the castle – indeed, from anywhere apart from the Haven itself. A watchtower up on top of the ridge, from where both the Haven and the castle would have been visible, would have been far more feasible.

Quite possibly the tower was a monastic establishment of some type, maybe even linked to the Knights Hospitallers, a well known religious brotherhood. As they possessed an establishment at Slebech as early as the twelfth century, it remains a possibility. There is no proof but, significantly, the name Llanreath was given to a nearby hill, at the western

A close-up view of Paterchurch Tower. Despite the dockyard walls that were soon to enclose it, the old building retains its air of ruined grandeur, even today.

end of the ridge, that divides Pembroke from Pembroke Dock. Llan is the Welsh word for church. Interestingly, however, the Royal Commission on Ancient Monuments, reporting in 1925, was adamant in its belief that, despite the statement by Pembrokeshire historian Fenton in 1810, this was never an ecclesiastical building. As far as they were concerned it was probably a fortified manor house, nothing more.

What is known is that by the fifteenth century, the tower was occupied by David de Patrickchurch, a Norman knight. By this time a substantial house was attached to the tower, providing living quarters for de Patrickchurch and his family. In 1422, following the marriage of Ellen de Patrickchurch and John Adams, the tower and house passed into the ownership of the Adams family. The family was still in occupation towards the end of the eighteenth century, the last reference to them as 'the Adams of Paterchurch' being made in 1731. Within a short period they had moved to their principal residence at Hollyland to the east of Pembroke and the old tower and its accompanying house were left without purpose or reason.

The tower changed hands once again in 1806 when it came into the possession of the Meyrick family, the principal landowners in the area. The house, known as Paterchurch Mansion, was then unoccupied and in a state of considerable disrepair.

The poorly defended state of Milford Haven had, for many years, been a source of some concern. It was, after all, an easy spot for any potential invader to disembark troops and water his supplying or supporting fleet. Numerous discussions and Parliamentary debates took place across the years, urgent recommendations to fortify the waterway being made on several occasions. Thomas Cromwell, the ruthlessly efficient advisor to Henry VIII, was one of the first to suggest that the area needed defending but he fell from power and went to the scaffold before anything could be done.

By the seventeenth century the only defensive work to have been completed in the area was the building of an armed camp at Pill, close to the future town of Milford. This had been created during the early years of the Civil War but the camp was destroyed when Parliamentary general Rowland Laugharne attacked it in February 1644. Laugharne is best remembered as one of the defenders of Pembroke Castle during the Second Civil War of 1648. Having conveniently changed sides, he and John Poyer held Cromwell at bay for several weeks before being starved into submission. Following his successful completion of the siege Cromwell ordered Pembroke Castle to be destroyed. Several towers and parts of the outer wall were blown down and thereafter the castle and the surrounding area subsided or lapsed into a relatively untroubled existence.

As far as defending the Haven was concerned, little more was done until the middle decade of the eighteenth century. The area still retained its strategic significance, however, and following the outbreak of war with France in 1756, Lt Colonel Bastide, Director of Engineers, surveyed the waterway and the surrounding countryside. Bastide's report suggested that six forts should be built along the sides of the Haven. It would have been an awesome sight, making the progress of enemy ships up Milford Haven virtually impossible.

Interestingly, the Parliamentary Report, that was compiled and presented, following Lt Colonel Bastide's report, commented that:

> If it should be thought proper hereafter ever to establish a Yard and Docks for the building and equipping of Fleets at Milford no place can, from Nature, Situation, Sail and general Concurrence of all necessary local circumstances be more fitted for such a design.

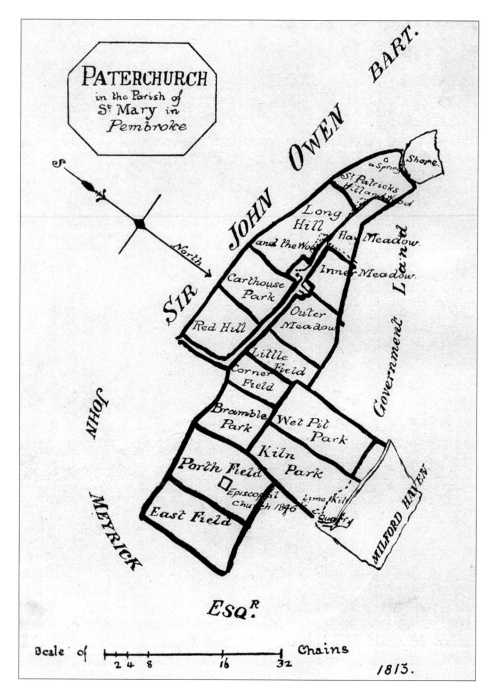

In light of future developments in the Haven and at the towns of Milford and Pembroke Dock such comments make interesting reading.

However, despite the very real threat of invasion, Bastide's recommendations were rejected as being too expensive and an alternative plan was put forward. This consisted of building just three forts, to be situated at the

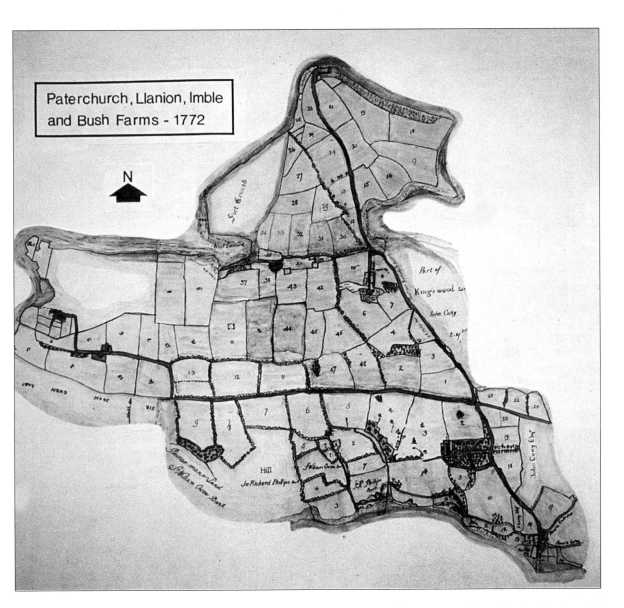

Paterchurch, Llanion, Imble and Bush Farms - 1772

N

Another early map showing Paterchurch, Llanion, Imble and Bush Farms, dating from approximately 1772. In those days the area consisted only of idyllic pasture lands.

landward end of the Haven, close to the future site of Pembroke dockyard. The forts were to be sited at Paterchurch Point, a mere stone's throw from the old Paterchurch Tower, at Llanion Point, half a mile to the east, and at Neyland Point, just across the river.

Land was duly purchased and the Ordnance Department drew up plans. In the event, the forts at Llanion and Neyland Points were never begun but work did actually commence on the proposed fortification at Paterchurch. By 1759, however, the danger from invasion had declined and work on the fort promptly ceased.

By 1812, then, all that broke the rolling expanse of hill, river and meadow at the eastern end of the Haven were the squat bulk of Paterchurch Tower and mansion, the ruins of the partially completed Ordnance Fort and a few isolated cottages, houses and barns. Most important of these was Paterchurch Farm, standing at the foot of the ridge and occupied by Francis White and his family. Within the space of a few short years, White had been forced off his land as the ever-developing dockyard and town were steadily extended. The way of life in the area changed out of all recognition as the quiet calm of Paterchurch Point was lost for ever.

CHAPTER TWO

The New Dockyard

W HEN LT COLONEL BASTIDE made his report on the defensive requirements of Milford Haven in 1757, he also carried out a survey of the waterway as a potential harbour. The Parliamentary Report that followed Bastide's investigations commented that the Committee had been informed:

> by several substantial ship-builders, who have built ships at Milford, that there cannot be a more proper place for building ships of any size than Barnlake.

Quite who these 'substantial ship-builders' were has never been made clear! Barnlake lay just up stream from Neyland and the comment was, in all probability, the result of a little judicious lobbying by local landowners who had spotted the potential to make money. Nevertheless, the area had been marked down for possible use as a ship building base at some stage, should the Navy need it.

It was not until the last few decades of the eighteenth century that events took a more definite turn. At that time Sir William Hamilton inherited land along the north shore of Milford Haven due to his marriage to Miss Wharton, an heiress of the Barlow family from Lawrenny. On the death of his wife, the aged Sir William retained his land along the Haven, located between Castle Pill and Hubberston Pill, and also acquired a new wife – the infamous Emma Hamilton.

Hamilton's Pembrokeshire lands were administered by his nephew and heir, the Hon. Charles Francis Greville. Hamilton and Greville were not just relatives. Greville had previously engaged in a long-term affair with the lady who now became his aunt and, in due course, had passed her on to Sir William. Clearly a very capable and gifted administrator, as well as someone with an eye towards his own future prospects, Greville advanced several ideas or schemes for developing the area. One of them was the foundation of a new town. It was a scheme that Sir William Hamilton seized on with alacrity.

It was not just a town that was being planned. Greville and Hamilton also intended to create an important port on the Haven and, to this end, by the late 1780s a packet service had been established between Hakin and Waterford in Ireland. In 1790 the Milford Haven Harbour Act was passed and, by 1792, the first plans for the new town were laid. That same year Greville was able to encourage a group of American Quaker whalers, who had been driven from Nantucket by the American War of Independence, to settle in the new community. His greatest gamble, however, was still to come.

Greville and Hamilton next established a private shipyard in the new town and leased it to a certain Mr Jacob. Embroiled in the long-running Revolutionary Wars with France, the Royal Navy urgently needed ships and in 1796 the Navy Board contracted Jacob to build three vessels, one

Charles Greville, from a portrait by George Romney. If one man can be said to have spawned Pembroke Dock then, arguably, that distinction belongs to Greville.

Milford Haven, a steel engraving by Bartholamew. The inset plan shows the new dockyard and town of Pembroke Dock.

of them a 74-gun ship of the line. She was to be followed by a frigate and a sloop. Importantly, the dockyard at Milford was never a Royal Navy yard, it was simply a rented or leased establishment. A Frenchman, Jean-Louis Barrallier from Toulon, was brought in to act as chief builder, with his son Charles as his assistant. Barrallier, incidentally, also built the first houses in the town of Milford, signing many of the early leases on behalf of Greville and Sir William Hamilton.

At that time the navy was effectively run by two separate and autonomous – not to say mutually antagonistic – organisations, the Navy Board and the Admiralty Board. The Navy Board was responsible for the supplying and provisioning of ships while the Admiralty Board operated the fleet. Dockyards were the responsibility of the Navy Board, a notoriously inefficient department.

While the navy, clearly, needed as many warships as it could lay its hands on, it is hard to understand quite why the town of Milford was chosen for this venture. Building yards in the nineteenth century required huge quantities of timber, pitch and spar wood – apparently it took over two thousand trees to build a ship like Nelson's *Victory* – and after the loss of the American colonies these supplies came from a variety of different sources. There was some use of Welsh oak but this was always a rather limited supply. The Forest of Dean also provided much of the necessary wood but Gloucestershire lay a long distance away and transport of heavy, bulky materials to the distant west was never easy. One of the major sources of supply was the Baltic and that, of course, was even further away. The Haven was, admittedly, a fine natural harbour but strategically it was not well positioned

Dockyards needed to be located on a suitable piece of flat land situated close to deep water where ships could be easily launched. Milford had neither. In addition, there was no pool of skilled labour in the area and communications with London were slow and tortuous. So Milford seemed then, and now, to be a strange place to create a new dockyard.

Viewed on these terms it soon becomes apparent that somebody had used his influence in order to get the new dockyard – and, as a consequence, the new town – up and running. And that person was probably Admiral Horatio Nelson.

It was not unusual for men in positions of power to use their personal influence in those days. Nelson had visited the town of Milford, his triumphant tour of Wales finishing at the hotel that now bears his name, in 1802. It is highly likely that he canvassed the Navy Board on behalf of his 'dearest Emma' and her cuckolded husband with whom he lived in a bizarre ménage à trois.

Whether or not this speculation is true cannot now be confirmed but there is little doubt that Nelson's 1802 visit was arranged in order to promote the project. The fact that the building of Milford's three ships continued after the Peace of Amiens in 1801 would seem to indicate that the visit was a success.

Mr Jacob went bankrupt at about this time but, once hostilities against France recommenced, the Navy Board promptly leased the dockyard on an annual basis and laid plans to build several more ships. In 1809, four years after Nelson's death, they embarked on a scheme to purchase the yards and, following a survey of the area by Mr E. Hall, Assistant to the Civil Architect and Engineer, to extend it along the front of the town. An Order in Council was prepared, dated 11 October, for the purchase of the dockyard and the creation of a Royal Dockyard. The proposed purchase price was £4,455. Barrallier was to stay on as chief builder, an acknowledgement that, although Nelson's sailors had consistently defeated the French, such success was due solely to superior seamanship. The art of ship building in Britain was far inferior to that practised on the Continent and this was clearly an opportunity to avail the country of superior French skills.

Again, the decision to purchase the Milford yard at this time was strange. Nelson's victory at Trafalgar had, effectively, ended the war at sea and the need for new ships was not as great as it had been five or six years before. Perhaps the Admiralty Board was attempting to create a 'model' dockyard under what Commander J. S. Guard has called:

> imported expert management, free of the hidebound traditions, stultifying conservatism and legendary corruption of the established Royal dockyards.

It is an interesting possibility but, whatever the reason, events now took a rather different turn. Negotiations were well under way when, on 23 April 1809, Charles Greville suddenly died. His estates, the very land that had once been owned by Sir William Hamilton, passed to Robert Fulke Greville, the brother of Charles. Negotiations had to begin again and the demands of the new landowner were considered exorbitant.

The proposed purchase of the Milford dockyard was promptly abandoned, despite the fact that improvements in the facilities were underway and Barrallier was already engaged in building two 74-gun warships in the yards. The decision had been made. The dockyard would move and the Navy Board did not have to look far for an alternative location.

The Ordnance already owned land at Paterchurch Point, six miles up the Haven and, unlike the site at Milford, it was considered to be very suitable for shipbuilding. When the Master Shipwright of the Milford yards, William Stone, inspected the area at the beginning of 1810 he found a flat, sheltered shelf of land adjacent to a stretch of deep water. It was, according to James Anderson Findley, an area of

> broad fields and fertile meadows … against which waters splashed their ceaseless spray in undisturbed tranquillity.

The area was surveyed by John Rennie between 24 and 29 September 1810 and notice of intent to move from Milford given to Greville on 2 August 1811. The land at Pater was easily transferred from the Ordnance to the Admiralty and Pembroke Dock's hundred year long history of shipbuilding had begun.

The area had already been marked down as a potential site for building ships. Charles Greville had once rented a piece of land close to the ruins of the partially completed Ordnance fort and he had actually applied for permission to build a dock there. He got as far as gathering together stones for the project but the lease was never granted and the proposal went no further.

An early view of the dockyard, this one showing the huge bulk of Pater Fort, just outside the walls.

There was much more space here than at Milford but, other than that, the area had almost as many drawbacks. Communications remained a problem and, most worrying of all, whatever skilled labour was now available was located several miles away down the Haven.

Despite these difficulties the Navy Board set to work, full of determination to make the new venture a success. The old frigate *Lapwing* was driven ashore, her purpose being to act as temporary accommodation, and officers were appointed to the establishment. Work began on four frigates and a much larger 74-gun ship.

However, there was something of a problem in these early days as there had been no Order in Council, authorising the setting up of the new yard. It meant that all of the appointments were, strictly speaking, illegal. How the Navy Board got around this has never been made clear. It is quite possible that, with the *Lapwing* still officially on the roll of the navy, officers were appointed to her. However it was done, the new yards were already busily working away while the old ones at Milford were still finishing off their last ships.

It soon became obvious that the new dockyard, covering just 20 acres, was not big enough and that more land would be needed. Consequently, on 10 March 1813, John Meyrick agreed to sell the Navy Board an additional four fields to the east of the embryo dockyard. He received the

This sketch of the dockyard by Mr C Norris dates from 1817. Just three years after the yard's first ships were launched, the dockyard wall is already in place and the first covered building shed has been erected.

sum of £3,000 – a huge sum of money in those days – but following an inspection by the Comptroller of the Navy and John Rennie it was decided that still more land would be needed. Accordingly, the Ordnance surrendered a further 39 acres and on 28 April 1814 another 20 acres, including a stream, were bought from John and Thomas Meyrick. Their boat had, literally, come in!

The wards of Pembroke and Pater are shown in this 1836 map by Dawson. At this stage the town of Pembroke was still considerably larger than nearby Pembroke Dock.

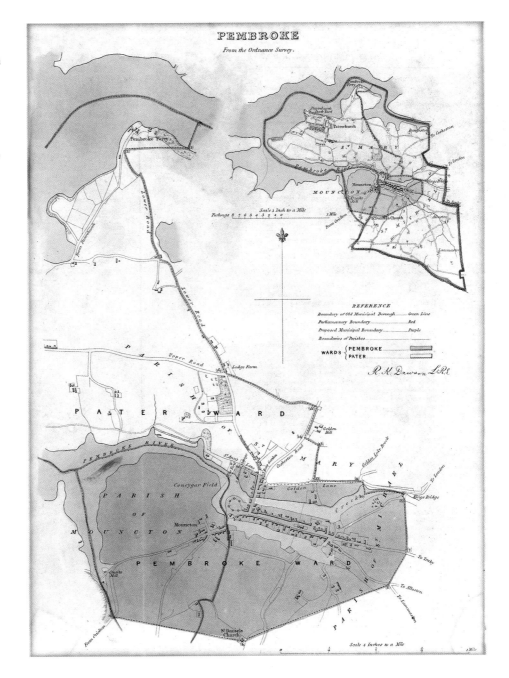

Pembroke Dockyard & Milford Haven.

It has to be asked why the Navy Board was quite so keen to establish the yards at Pater. They had paid out vast sums of money to the Meyrick family – and were soon to pay even more, both to the Meyricks and to other local landowners. Following the British victory at the Battle of Waterloo in 1815 peace came once more to Europe. And with peace came an automatic reduction in the size of the armed forces. Closure of a dockyard that had not really begun its work would have been a logical way to proceed – particularly when, technically speaking, the place did not exist.

Yet, despite these perfectly reasonable reasons for economy, the Navy Board went the other way. An Order in Council was presented on 31 October 1815, outlining the reasons for the move from Milford to Pater and the need to purchase more land. The Order concluded with the following passage:

> And having since deemed it expedient for the good of His Majesty's Service to direct the formation of a dockyard on the said land at Pater, according to a plan proposed to us by the Comptroller of the Navy and Mr Rennie … being of an opinion that it will be necessary to appoint officers and clerks, many of whom we have found it necessary to appoint provisionally for the purpose of superintending the building of a 74-gun ship, two 5th and two 6th rates now building there.

Was that a case of the members of the Navy Board covering their backs, perhaps? The Order in Council went on to establish Pater as a Royal Dockyard and listed the officers who were to take up appointment. Interestingly, Jean-Louis Barrallier was not included. He had been replaced by a Navy Board Master Shipwright, Mr Stone, and it was this man who took over the responsibility of the new yard.

There is a theory that the Admiralty Board, mindful of the hatred felt by Lord Nelson and all sea-going officers towards the Navy Board – these serving sailors had, after all, been victims of the Board's inefficiency – was attempting to breathe new life into the traditional dockyard system. That was why they agreed to the yards at Milford, in a location that was never really suitable for shipbuilding, employing a brand new labour force under experts like Barrallier who were brought in from outside the system. The Admiralty Board, goes the theory, simply used the creation of the Milford dockyard to obtain the site they really wanted at Paterchurch Point.

It is an interesting argument but, at this distance, there is no proof. What is clear, however, is that the Admiralty Board failed in its plan – if, indeed, such a plan ever existed – in the face of the powerful vested interests of the Navy Board. The price of the Navy Board's co-operation was that their men must be in charge of the dockyard at Pater. So the unfortunate Jean-Louis Barrallier went to the wall and the first officers in the yards were traditional Navy Board men.

These were dynamic and difficult times for the dockyard and the area. Mrs Peters, in her seminal book on the history of the town, tells the story of the first marking out of the new yards:

> in the first boatload that came up the Haven to plug out the yards, one man, named Owen, leaped on the shore first, exclaiming, as he placed a plug in the ground, 'Here goes one for the first ship.'

Whether the story is true or apocryphal hardly matters. The image and the sentiment seem to fit the mood of expansion and of 'carving out' new territory. On 17 April 1814 the *Rochefort*, the last Milford ship, was finally launched and the whole establishment transferred to the yards at Pater.

One of the first problems encountered at the new dockyard was the lack of suitable labour in the immediate area. Such specialist labour that existed was only to be found in the town of Milford, a good six miles away downstream. For a while many of the workmen travelled to Pater each day, rowing up and down the stormy waters of the Haven at all states of the tide. It must have been a hard pull for the oarsmen and, having reached the dockyard each morning, there would be the mind-numbing prospect of a full days work ahead. In the evening would come another row back down the Haven.

It was clear that at some stage in the not too distant future houses would have to be built, close to the dockyard, for the workmen and their families. The men could certainly not continue to row up and down the Haven each day. However, that was something that would have to wait. For the moment the Navy Board had more pressing matters to deal with.

The dockyard had been surrounded by a low picket fence since it was first marked out in 1812. This made it far too easy for workmen to climb out and for inquisitive strangers to get in. So, in 1814, boundary walls were built at the eastern and western ends of the dockyard by a contractor called Isaacs. The southern extremities were left open for several years.

Reportedly, the first stone of the original wall was laid by David Price, who also happened to be one of the first men ashore to mark out the yards. Price later kept the Dolphin public house in Llanreath and died in 1894, aged 97 years. The original dockyard wall was pulled down in the years after 1830 and the huge 12 foot structure that still dominates the western edge of the town was built in its place.

The dockyard begins to take regular shape in this painting by an unknown artist. Notice the ruins of Paterchurch Mansion in the foreground.

It appears to be rather a blustery day in this artist's impression of the dockyard, circa 1850. Considerable licence has been taken by the artist – notice, for example, the fronts of the building sheds that here seem to be totally enclosed.

To begin with, conditions in the dockyard were crude in the extreme. There were a few workmen's sheds, the old *Lapwing* – although the comfort afforded by her leaking decks was probably reserved solely for the officers – and the smithy's shop. Apart from that, there was little shelter for anyone.

Working in the new dockyard in these early days must have been a cold and thankless task. Certainly working conditions were far from comfortable. The carpenters and shipwrights often toiled up to their waists in mud and water and the only protection from the driving rain and wind would have come from a piece of sacking or canvas draped around their shoulders.

The first four ships were all laid down, built and launched in the open air. By the time that the dockyard was formally established by the Order in Council in 1815, construction of the first four ships was already well under way and, only a few months later, on 10 February 1816, the yard's first two ships were launched. The *Ariadne* and *Valorous*, 28-gun frigates, slipped into the quiet waters of Milford Haven, the first in a long line of famous and distinguished vessels to be launched from the yards at Pembroke Dock.

CHAPTER THREE

Growing Bigger

OVER THE NEXT TWENTY years the dockyard and the town, which soon sprang up around its walls, developed and grew at a phenomenal rate. Interestingly, the first hydrographic survey of the yards did not take place until 1832 when Lieutenant Denham came to carry out the task. By then the name Pater had been dropped and the town was already becoming known as Pembroke Dock.

The survey showed buildings and slipways that were planned for the years ahead as well as those already in existence. Development was obviously proceeding according to the plan proposed by the Comptroller of the Navy and John Rennie in the 1815 Order in Council. By 1832 much of that plan was already in existence and future developments showed little or no deviation from the original intentions.

Houses to accommodate the dockyard workforce were begun soon after the yards were established. Many of them were single storey cottages like this one and are still a unique feature in many Pembroke Dock streets.

By now the yards had been extended several times. On 22 January 1822 a further 37 acres of land had been bought from the Meyrick family and a few months later another 51 acres were purchased from Sir John Owen, the other major landowner in the region. This latter purchase included the southern part of what was then called 'the Furzy' but which later became known as the Barrack Hill. This was the time when farmer Francis White lost what little remained of his land in the area as his landlords eagerly seized the money offered by the Navy Board. The hill overlooking the dockyard was the western extremity of the ridge which divided the new town from Pembroke and the Pembroke River.

This new purchase of land soon proved to have little or no value for the dockyard however, and in 1830, in exchange for a further 13 acres surrendered by the Ordnance, closer to the yards, the Admiralty gave up to the military all the land it had purchased in 1822. This land eventually provided the army with its bases on the Barrack Hill and at Pennar.

To begin with, most of the ship building was carried out in the eastern part of the dockyard but as its importance grew the slips were gradually extended westwards. Building sheds were soon erected over the slipways, the cutter *Racer* of 1818 being the first vessel to be totally built under cover.

The gradual extension of the yards to the west did not reach completion until 1851 when the yard's dry dock was also extended. One of the famous old 'legends' of the town dates from this period. The dockyard wall had to be extended around the new land and this involved closing off the ruins of Paterchurch Tower and a small, two-roomed cottage occupied by a woman called Ann Jones. Known as Nanny Herring, she used to sell beer and biscuits to the workmen in their breaks, marking up their purchases on the wall of her cottage. Settlement of the bills came on pay day and woe betide anyone who failed to clear their slate. Nanny Herring was relocated into another house on the slopes of Llanreath, close to a fresh water spring. For many years the place was known as Nanny Herring's Well.

Royal Marines had been appointed to guard the dockyard from its early days. They were accommodated in an old wooden-wall called the *Dragon* which was run up onto the shingle close to the yards. The *Dragon* also acted as a schoolroom for dockyard apprentices. Here they were taught their skills under the watchful eyes of the first schoolmaster, Mr Good, until more suitable premises were found for them above one of the dockyard storehouses.

The town itself began to take shape soon after the creation of the dockyard. Mapped out on a uniform north–south, east–west grid pattern of almost mathematical accuracy, the streets and houses soon mushroomed along the flat shore of the Haven.

Mrs Peters, in *The History of Pembroke Dock*, quotes from the diary of John Narbeth, a carpenter who was one of the first tradesmen to work on building the new houses of the town. It makes fascinating reading:

> On the 14th day of May 1814, Mr Lowless and myself left poor old Pembroke to commence its rival town. So on that day was the first shaving cut and the first window frame made by John Narbeth; and by Sept. 25th 1814, were the first four houses made ready. Mrs Thomas, the foreman of shipwright's wife, came that day to take possession.

These first four houses were built in Front Street, originally called Thomas Street after Sir Thomas Meyrick. They were completed, as John Narbeth confirmed, by the early autumn of 1814 and, in all probability, were the houses that are now numbered 25 to 28 Front Street. There is no hard, factual proof for that statement but, in looking for the first four houses, it is logical to look for buildings of similar construction. Numbers

The first houses in the town were built in Front Street. This modern view shows Nos 25 to 28, in all probability the first actual houses. Despite modification and the raising of the upstairs windows in No 26 they are clearly of a similar, uniform design.

25 to 28 certainly fit that bill. In addition, these first properties were not leased but built for John Meyrick, on land that he owned close to the dockyard, previously known as Kiln Park, so that he could then rent them out. No leases exist for 25 to 28 Front Street, thus making them favourites for the honour of being the first houses in the new town.

The first houses were occupied by dockyard officials like Mr Thomas, the foreman shipwright, and by Mr Clun, the storeman for the new establishment. Another large property was soon built for Mr Stone, the Master Shipwright, and with the need to build houses for the workforce now becoming increasingly clear, leases were soon granted for Numbers 29, 30 and 31 Front Street. Between August 1814 and 2 January 1815 land was leased to build a further fifteen homes in the street. The town's first public house was quickly created on the west corner of King Street. This roadway was originally known as Middle Street and, being begun in 1816, was the second of the town's streets to be formed. It was followed by Queen Street, Upper Street as it was then called, Commercial Row, running adjacent to the dockyard wall, and Bellevue Terrace. This road was, from the earliest days, more commonly known as Tregenna's Hill, so called after Mr Tregenna who may or may not have had Cornish connections and lived in a large house at the top of the steep slope.

The town's development in these early years followed a logical progression, moving steadily inland from the river. They were broad streets that followed the line of the stream or, as in the case of Tregenna's Hill, cut a wide swathe up the side of the overlooking ridge. Clarence Street,

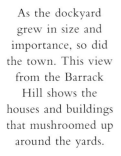

As the dockyard grew in size and importance, so did the town. This view from the Barrack Hill shows the houses and buildings that mushroomed up around the yards.

Brewery Street and Park Street were all built in 1827 while in 1830 a start was made on Melville Street and Market Street. Interestingly, at this time Clarence Street was more commonly called Friday Street, due to the habit of market traders in the nearby market leaving their carts there on Fridays, traditionally the market day for the town.

STILL IN 1950's

The Albion Square complex, close to the dockyard walls, was completed in the 1830s on land that had once been farmed by Francis White and his family. Designed around a wide, open area, the complex later grew to include Albion Square Congregational Church (better known as the Tabernacle) in 1867 and Albion Square School in 1877. The name of the square owes its origin to the Albion House brewery which stood here for many years.

In the late 1840s Meyrick Street, Bush Street, Lewis Street and Laws Street were all developed while yet more houses were built at Pennar, on the southern slope of the ridge overlooking the town. Until the development of Pennar, the only other outlying district of the town had been Pembroke Ferry. This was an old settlement to the east of the town and had, for many years, been the site of the main ferry between south and north Pembrokeshire. Lord Cawdor had crossed the Cleddau at this point when he marched to Fishguard to defeat the French Légion Noire who had landed in the county in February 1797, the last time that mainland Britain was ever invaded. John Wesley used the ferry on many occasions, as did General Picton on his way to Belgium and death and immortality on the field of Waterloo.

Albion Square Congregational Church, now long demolished.

Dimond Street was not, to begin with, the main shopping centre for the town but over the years it gradually assumed that role from Bush Street and Commercial Row. This view shows the old W H Smith and Sons newsagents shop that used to stand in the street with its original entrance in adjacent Meyrick Street.

DIMOND STREET, PEMBROKE DOCK

The Swan Inn at Pennar was, for many years, regarded as the cleanest and best-kept public house in the town. Yet the village or community of Pennar itself was far from healthy. The houses lacked clean water supplies and decent sewerage arrangements and the inevitable result was a serious cholera epidemic in 1865–66. Many deaths were reported.

Within the main part of the town, Queen Street West soon became known as Officers Row, as this was where many of the dockyard officials and officers took lodgings. The origins of some of the street names are interesting. Brewery Street derives its name from the adjacent brewery in Albion Square while the name Prospect Place, which dates from the 1830s, has a fairly obvious origin as the road faces the Haven and has glorious views across the waterway. Dimond Street is not so obvious. The street, now the main shopping area for the town, was developed piece-meal. The north side of the road was, for several years, only a thorny hedge while the south side was built and developed some fifteen years earlier. Quite why the spelling should choose to omit the letter 'a' is not clear.

Dockyard workers of the time – not to mention the soldiers whose job it was to protect them – were notoriously 'thirsty' individuals and so it is no surprise to learn that the public houses and beer shops of the town did a roaring trade. By 1850 there were nearly 60 hostelries in Pembroke Dock, many of them small drinking dens which were allowed by law until the Wine and Beer-house Act of 1869 effectively closed them down. At the time of the Act, Front Street, barely a quarter of a mile in length, had as many as ten pubs while King Street was more than liberally endowed with up to fifteen ale houses.

A typical building plot in the town measured approximately 100 ft by 25 ft and over half of the houses enjoyed the luxury of a narrow service lane to the rear. The roads and streets were, and remain, incredibly wide and elegant. The reason for the, perhaps, excessive width of the roadways was partly to allow the easy passage of heavy materials bound for the dock-yard and partly so that the populace of the new town could bask in the splendour of elegant buildings and walkways.

The story of the town's streets is not always so splendid, however. Bush Street, one of the main thoroughfares, was once known by the inelegant term Pigs Parade! Closures and shut-downs in other dockyards during the 1840s resulted in a sudden and unexpected influx of men, desperate for work, to Pembroke Dock. And there was

Crowds of workmen leave by the main dockyard gate at the end of a day's work in the yards.

Bush Street was, for a long time, the main centre of commerce in Pembroke Dock. But it was not always so important or so well-groomed. At one stage in the street's history it was so dirty and run down that it was known as Pigs Parade

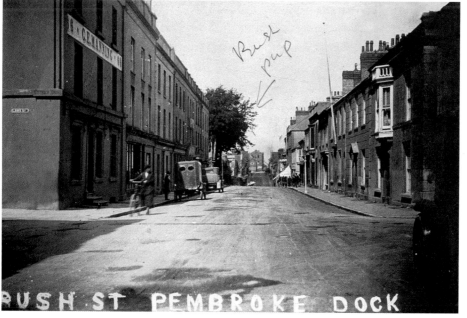

Hobbs Point and the town are shown here in an 1861 print taken from *Mr and Mrs Hall's Tour of South Wales and the Wye.*

simply not enough accommodation available in the town. Consequently, many of the new arrivals were forced to live in hastily erected shacks and tin sheds along the edge of Bush Street. Living conditions were squalid, hence the name Pigs Parade.

While most of the houses in the town were built on a regular grid pattern consisting, in the main, of two storey buildings, there were – and still are – exceptions. Most notable of these are the terraced rows of single storey workmen's cottages built along High Street on the top of the ridge on the main road to Pembroke and in quiet backwaters like Owen Street and Military Road in Pennar. They remain a distinctive feature of Pembroke Dock.

The foundation stone of Hobbs Point pier was laid in 1830, the excavations for the jetty having begun the year before. Work finished in 1832 at a cost of £20,250. An enormous diving bell used to help in the construction was regarded as one of the wonders of the modern world and, for several months, was a source of great amusement and entertainment for dockyard workers and their families. The name Hobbs Point probably derives from Nicholas Hobbs who once owned land in the area but, as he died in 1728, this is mere speculation. Before Hobbs Point was opened, private passengers and freight had to be conveyed to Pembroke Ferry, a mile further upstream, rather inconvenient if your destination was the town of Pembroke Dock.

Building the pier was a Government sponsored scheme, the main object being to develop the packet service from the Haven to southern Ireland. In 1836 the sailing packets that had previously worked out of Milford were diverted to Hobbs Point in order to meet the Mail Coaches which now ran daily from the new pier. In due course these sailing vessels were replaced by small steamers like the *Adder, Jasper, Prospero* and *Viper* which became common sights on the Haven.

For the next few tempestuous and exciting years Pembroke Dock experienced the true glory of the old coaching era. These were the days when the Mail Coaches clattered busily along London Road, heading to and from the Royal, the coaching inn and stables that had been built close to Hobbs Point. Sarah Williams, the landlady of the Royal, became the town's post-mistress. It does not take the greatest imagination in the world to picture the scene. With snorting horses, blaring coach horns and drivers muffled to the chin in voluminous coats and giant scarves it has to have been an image worthy of Dickens himself.

Another print from the same book, this shows the yards and building slips.

In these late days of the stage coach era the mail coaches did not make the run all the way to London. They went only to Gloucester, still a trip of two or three days, and there met the London train to transfer passengers, parcels and letters. Regular stops and halts along the way meant that the drivers and horses could be changed regularly. Pembroke Dock drivers tended to go only as far as St Clears, usually returning with the next in-coming coach. The most famous of these drivers was called Bramble, supposedly a great character who later hung himself in a fit of depression once the coaching service was ended.

By 1848, with the railway now reaching as far as Clynderwen, the writing was on the wall for the stage coaches and the Royal Mail service was suspended. After the railway was extended to Neyland (New Milford as it was known) the mails and passengers were ferried easily across the waterway from Hobbs Point and sent by train to their destination. The old Royal was closed and, in due course, handed over to the Coastguard Service.

The demise of the Royal Mail coaches did not spell the absolute end of coaching in Pembroke Dock. Ordinary coaches hung on for a while longer, starting and finishing their journeys outside the old Victoria Hotel at the top of Pembroke Street. Across the road from the Victoria stood the Clarence Inn. One of the weekly arrivals brought the London paper to the town and Mrs Peters has gone on record as saying that:

Alderman Hughes of Bush Street used to stand on the steps of the Clarence Inn and read the paper to the people who congregated there for the purpose of hearing it every Sunday. During the Crimean War a crowd collected long before the arrival of the coach on the newspaper day, anxious to hear the latest news.

After the closure of the Royal at Hobbs Point, the Clarence served as the town's post office. The landlord, George Husband, was the postmaster and remained so for the next 25 years. He eventually gave up his job as a publican and moved to the new premises when a purpose-built post office was created in Meyrick Street in 1869.

The people of Pembroke and Pembroke Dock were not slow to realise the value of Hobbs Point as a jetty. Almost from the beginning it was used as a landing place for ferry boats and similar traffic, applications for such use having to be made to the Government. Once a year, a rope was placed across the access road in order to preserve the Government's rights of ownership and to emphasise that access to the pier and use of it were Government gifts to give.

While the town was originally known as Pater, it was a name that did not stick. At one time there was a suggestion that the new community should be called Melvillestown, in honour of the First Lord of the

The dockyard is shown here in the mid nineteenth century – lots of activity in the yards and on the waterway.

Pembroke Dock Yard

Pembroke Street
with the Haven
beyond. A three
funnelled cruiser
lies alongside Hobbs
Point, ready to be
fitted out.

Admiralty. Nothing came of the proposal. The name Pembroke Dock was a logical one as the new town was situated close to its medieval namesake and it did, as a matter of course, provide dockyard services. Almost by accident the name seems to have been accepted, the Admiralty itself soon addressing mail and goods to 'Pembroke Docks'.

In these early years workmen flocked to the new town and dockyard. Many of them came from the other Royal Dockyards. The Admiralty made several calls for volunteers in order to develop the new yards and workers came with their families from places as far away as Portsmouth, Devonport, Chatham and Woolwich. Others came from the country areas of Pembrokeshire as work in the dockyard, and in the growing community based around it, offered the chance of a better life and better standard of living.

As the town grew in size it became more and more important that a proper burial ground should be created. Many early inhabitants were interred in Monkton churchyard, outside Pembroke, others in the grave-yard of the original Bethany Chapel. However, it was soon decided that the town needed its own special place for burials.

The Meyrick family of Bush House donated a small piece of land in South Park Street and on 26 September 1834 the Bishop of St David's consecrated the area as a burial ground. The first interment was of a man called Instance, a rather appropriate name, on 11 October 1834. Local legend declares that Instance was one of the men working on the graveyard wall. Apparently, as he put the finishing touches to the job, he looked up and declared 'That's finished. I wonder who'll be first to be buried here, then?'

In the early days of the town the Admiralty maintained an almost fatherly approach to the growing community. The dockyard wall had enclosed the landing place used by local people and so the Admiralty built what was soon called 'the Common Hard' in Front Street as a form of recompense. In addition to this, the huge Admiralty reservoir, situated at the foot of Tregenna's Hill, provided both the dockyard and those streets nearest to the yards with a limited supply of fresh water.

Above all, however, it soon became clear that the town needed a market. And so, in about 1818, the Admiralty or, rather, the Navy Board of the Admiralty, proposed to build one. Things were not that simple, however. By ancient charter the sole right to trade within the Borough of Pembroke – which then included the new town of Pembroke Dock – was reserved for the Freemen of Pembroke. The Mayor of Pembroke, Anthony Stokes, raised strong objections to the proposal and the matter was put on hold.

Pembroke Dock on Market Day, traditionally always a Friday. The Market Hall was built for the town by the Admiralty in 1826.

For over six years discussion and debate raged before, finally, the Navy Board was given permission to build its market house. In addition to the cost of the building, they had to pay £3000 in compensation for the breaching of their monopoly to the Freemen of Pembroke. The total cost of the project was over £4630 and the market house was not completed until 1826.

The people of Pembroke were, apparently, overjoyed at the successful conclusion of the case and balls and other festivities were promptly held to celebrate. As Commander J. S. Guard has commented:

> Having pocketed their share, presumably the Freemen who so wished then proceeded to trade in the new market!

Compared with other towns that grew up around commercial operations during the Industrial Revolution there is no doubt that the Admiralty were caring and careful landlords and employers. The Act authorising the Navy Board to establish the market in Pembroke Dock was passed on 2 July 1819 and charged them to make regulations for the paving, lighting and good order of the town. It placed the Navy Board in the clear role of 'founding father', as well as sole employer and municipal authority to the new community.

The dockyard officials, the men on the spot as it were, must take much of the credit for the compassionate way in which the new town was helped to grow and develop in these early years. People like Captain Savage of the Royal Engineers, who was Superintendent of Works, and Edward Laws, the Clerk of the Cheque and Storekeeper, were in post by 1830 and were hugely influential in the way that Pembroke Dock developed.

It was not all sweetness and light in these early years, however. Pembroke Dock was a rough, tough place to live and there is a distinctly 'Wild West' feel to some of the stories about the place. The Old Lion in King Street was a popular drinking haunt for soldiers and was also regularly frequented by many of the prostitutes who soon began to work in the town. After one wild evening in the pub, full of carousing and illicit affairs, the garrison commandant actually issued an order banning his troops from visiting the place. It hardly mattered to the soldiers. In King Street alone there were dozens of other drinking dens to choose from.

One of the King Street inns was known as The Ship on the Launch. It was renowned as a place where stolen goods were traded or sold. Fights regularly occurred on the premises and later, in 1850, magistrates took landlady Eliza Evans to court and closed the place down. According to

Keith Johnson in *The Pubs of Pembroke, Pembroke Dock, Tenby and South Pembrokeshire* it was a wild and exciting episode:

the court was packed with rowdy supporters of Eliza Evans who repeatedly directed 'unseemly and harsh remarks' at the bench.

Despite all this, there were many attempts at making the town a little more genteel. In these early days the local gentry, dockyard officials and army officers often came together to plan the social calendar and race meetings were sometimes held at the Redwell Race Course, on what was soon to be called the Barrack Hill. In 1830 a celebratory dinner was held at the Clarence Inn to mark the end of a particularly successful meeting. The inn was home to the town's freemasons for many years before they switched their lodge to the rather more up-market Victoria, situated just across the other side of the street. The Clarence continued to be known as the town's most radical house. As Keith Johnson has said:

The two large houses shown here at the top of Pembroke Street were the Clarence and Victoria, for a long while the most important and best-kept public houses in the town.

Since this was the meeting place of the local Reform Committee, any newspaper editorial opposed to the various Reform Acts would be roundly jeered; in 1832 a copy of the rabidly Tory Carmarthen Journal was publicly burnt, to the delight of the gathering outside the Clarence.

When the famous Reform Act of 1832 was passed, bringing to an end hundreds of years of government by privilege, it was the beginning of a series of wild celebrations in the Clarence.

Commercial Row became the first street in the town to be lit by gas and in the early 1850s there was an attempt to turn the area into a fashionable promenade. Trees were planted along the dockyard wall, benches were erected and military bands played as couples strolled easily along the length of the street. Quite what they made of the carousing soldiers and dockyard workers in the beer dens of King Street, barely a hundred yards away, is not known.

By 1830 there were 500 men employed in the dockyard. No Naval officers were appointed to the yard, all officers and employees being civilian men. Things were about to change, however. In 1832 the Navy Board and Admiralty Board were combined into one organisation under the Board of Admiralty. One significant outcome of this revolutionary change to naval operations was that Naval officers were now appointed to take charge of all Royal Dockyards. As a consequence of this, Pembroke Dockyard shortly received its first Captain Superintendent, Captain Charles Bullen, CB.

It must have been a worrying time for the established officers in the dockyard. People like Edward Laws, Clerk of the Cheque and Storekeeper, and Master Shipwright Thomas Roberts had only just moved into their newly completed houses. What would the future bring? Was the arrival of Bullen the beginning of the end for them?

In the event Laws and Roberts need not have worried. When Bullen arrived he found an establishment that was highly efficient and clearly justifying its position and reputation as the Navy's most modern dockyard. A regular building programme was in operation with a frigate or similar vessel being launched about once a year, a line-of-battle ship every three or four years. A steady stream of smaller vessels – lighters, cutters and sloops – filled the periods in between.

Some years saw several launches. In 1820, for example, no fewer than four ships slipped into the waters of Milford Haven. In 1829 there were five. Bullen was happy with what he saw. Laws, in particular, continued to work in the dockyard for another twenty-five years, dying in office as a well-respected local dignitary. He was even awarded the distinction of having one of the main roads in the town named after him.

By this time there were already twelve building slips in the dockyard – out of an eventual total of thirteen. By now, however, the original slip on which the *Ariadne* and *Valorous* had been built was outside the boundary wall and was, presumably, no longer in use. The graving dock, used to remove the launching cradles from newly built hulls, was also now up and running and the whole yard was a scene of great activity. Sawpits and storehouses, sheds and workshops, timber stacks and offices, gave the place an intense sense of purpose.

Along the southern dockyard wall the first of the elegant houses for dockyard officials were already in place. The Dockyard Chapel had been completed in 1831. Built by G.L. Taylor, architect to the Navy Board, it remains one of the finest examples of nineteenth century naval architecture. A beautiful stained glass window in the building, designed by Mr WH Churchward, Civil Engineer in the dockyard, was erected as a memorial to the officers and men who had lost their lives when HMS *Atalanta* sank with all hands.

Another memorial in the chapel was erected in honour of the indefatigable Edward Laws. It read as follows:

Sacred to the Memory of
Edward Laws, Esquire,
Who departed this life on the 2nd of January 1854, aged 62 years
And whose remains are deposited in a catacomb in
Kensal Green Cemetery, London.
This tablet is erected by permission of the Lords Commissioners
of the Admiralty, who expressed their regret at the loss the public
service had sustained by the death of one who had deservedly
possessed the entire confidence of every Board of Admiralty under
which he had served.
A principal officer in the Dockyard of his Sovereign at home and
abroad, for a period of nearly forty years. He was long a resident
in the Dockyard, where his worth and benevolence in private life
not only endeared him to his numerous friends, but obtained him
the respect and esteem of a large class of society in this and the
neighbouring counties.

The memorial was lost for many years after the closure of the dockyard but was eventually found, outside the chapel, smashed into dozens of pieces. It has now been put back together by members of the Pembroke Dock Museum Trust and can be seen in the museum premises in Dimond Street.

By 1832, then, the town and dockyard were well established. There was employment for everyone who wanted it and a growing sense of civic pride and dignity. It seemed as if the future was assured.

CHAPTER FOUR

Defending the Yards

Almost from the moment of its inception Pembroke Dock became a military town. Dockyards needed to be protected. After all, they were a valuable asset offering not just huge amounts of raw material and supplies but also ideal landing stages for any invading army. Deprive a country of its ability to make warships and you were well on the way towards reducing its fleet. Pembroke Dock and its new building yard were no different from any other dockyard.

The detachment of Royal Marines – perhaps as many as 500 of them – detailed to provide a guard for the dockyard arrived early in the history of the community. They were transferred from the Portsmouth Division and, as we have seen, were billeted in the old wooden warship *Dragon*. The Marines used to enter the dockyard through an opening in the eastern wall, carry out their duties and then return to the *Dragon* for their off-

The 12 foot dockyard wall that still exists in the town dates from circa 1832–44. The main entrance gate was built by Edward Hall, architect to the Navy Board, and boasted two elegant pillars with anchors on top. A chain with a lamp, clearly seen in this view, was slung between the pillars.

Dozens of different regiments served at Pembroke Dock over the years. This rare photograph, circa 1901, shows the 2nd Battalion Royal Northern Reserves drawn up on the parade ground of the old Hut Encampment.

duty hours. It was surely no accident that the town's first public house, the Globe – or the Albion as it was called at one stage – was located in the same general area as their barracks.

Within a few years of the dockyard's foundation it was realised that a small detachment of Marines would not be strong enough to keep a determined attack at bay. Therefore they were soon bolstered by the addition of two companies of the 14th West Yorkshire Regiment and Pembroke Dock's history as a garrison town had begun.

The old Pater Fort, despite never having been completed, was garrisoned for a short while but conditions in the old building were far from ideal. It was demolished in 1847 and the site given to the Admiralty so that the Dockyard Battalion could be properly exercised and trained.

The Pater Volunteer Artillery had been formed as early as 1840, the ranks being filled by dockyard workers who were paid a small sum to carry out defensive duties in addition to their ordinary work. However, in 1846 permission was granted (General Order No 586) to raise bodies of 'Dock Yard Corps' in the various Royal Naval yards across the country. The purpose behind the Dockyard Battalions was, as the name suggests, to help protect all the ports where dockyards were located but it was clearly intended to be defence 'on the cheap.' Only dockyard employees could be enrolled in the new force. In Pembroke Dock the Pater Volunteer Artillery stood down and the 8th Battalion, Royal Dockyard Corps was founded.

Most Dockyard Battalions – the title Royal was granted soon after their formation – trained solely as infantry but the Pembroke Dock Battalion was an artillery unit. It was a logical decision as the guns of the Pater Volunteer Artillery Corps were still mounted in Pater Fort and could be usefully employed in defence of the yards. Officers for the new Battalion were chosen from the heads of the various departments within the yard while the instructors were retired Marines. The Adjutant was a serving Royal Marine officer.

The names of some of the officers involved with the unit have come down to us, the two commanding officers being Colonel Gordon Thomas Falcon and Colonel Robert Smart. Both of them were ex Superintendents of the dockyard. Other officers included Majors George Chiles (better known as the dockyard Storekeeper) and Richard Bonniwell, Captains Richard Kneebone and John Davidson and the Adjutant, Lieutenant Walter Gillies. The unit's band was led by Mr Ribbon, father of William Ribbon who was, for many years, organist in the Royal Dockyard Chapel.

The Pembroke Dock Battalion, like other dockyard units, carried out its training exercises after working hours. An incentive payment of one shilling (5 pence) per parade was offered to every man who attended, a useful bonus on top of normal wages. The unit, although nominally on the strength of the army, was actually controlled by the navy. This was due to the fact that, until 1855, the Admiralty controlled all coastal defences throughout the country.

Uniforms were specially designed for the Pembroke Dock Battalion, a double-breasted tunic made from fine blue cloth with red collar and cuffs. Buttons were made from quilt and bore the inscription 'Royal Dock Yard Battn.' along with a fouled anchor and the cipher 'VR', and ran in two rows down the front of the tunic. The original headdress was a blue shako, later replaced by a spiked helmet. Officers carried a sword which bore the same inscription as the men's uniform buttons while the rank and file were armed with French percussion muskets – a fire having destroyed Britain's stockpile of reserve rifles a few years before – and a sword bayonet.

While the Battalion carried out most of its training in Pater Fort, during the summer months they would often head out of the dockyard to take part in field exercises. These activities were not always totally successful.

One infamous exercise took place in 1853 when the part-time soldiers were ferried across the Haven to land on the northern shore of the estuary, somewhere between Neyland Point and Church Lake. Thousands of spectators came to see the Dockyard Battalion carry out its manoeuvres in a field close to Great Honeyborough. The Battalion marched to the field accompanied by their Regimental Band and performed numerous foot and musket drills until three in the afternoon when they exercised with their field guns.

Several rounds were fired from the guns but, as the drills continued, a sudden thunderstorm broke out. Torrential rain lashed at the field and the spectators ran for cover – not that there was much available. The watching ladies, in particular, were left in a terrible state, most of them being dressed in light summer dresses. The review was abandoned and the Battalion headed off for the Haven to take their boats back to the dockyard. However, the fleeing crowd had churned the road into a quagmire. All semblance of order disappeared and the shout of 'Get to the boats as best you can' promptly went up. Chaos followed, a third of the Battalion not making it to the embarkation point with some soldiers eventually inexplicably finding themselves in far-off Haverfordwest – 'Dad's Army' indeed.

The various Royal Dockyard Corps lasted for just ten years when, in 1857, with the exception of the Malta Battalion, they were removed from the Army List. The Pembroke Dock Battalion was disbanded along with all the rest. There was an attempt to reform them in 1860 but it came to nothing and, that same year, the Pater Artillery Volunteers were reformed. They remained in service until 1884.

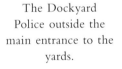

The Dockyard Police outside the main entrance to the yards.

Responsibility for the security of all Royal Naval Dockyards passed to the Metropolitan Police in the period 1860 – 61. Consequently, the 5th Division of the Metropolitan Police arrived to take over policing duties in Pembroke Dockyard on 17 December 1860. Prior to this the dockyard had its own police force. However, they were not a particularly efficient or well-run force as a renowned incident from 1849 shows. A letter in *The Pembrokeshire Herald* records that a visitor to the dockyard was received very politely by a smiling policeman who then showed him around the yards. Later in the day, the same policeman was seen offering contraband goods for sale.

The arrival of the 5th Division – the Dockyard Police as they were known – put an end to such practices. They were a totally separate force from the local constabulary and at their establishment in 1860 consisted of one Superintendent, two Inspectors, five Sergeants and 26 Constables.

In 1844 work began on the Defensible Barracks. High above the dockyard, on the top of what soon came to be called the Barrack Hill, these huge stone barracks are said to have been completed within a twelve month period. The contractor, Thomas Jackson, handed them over to the military on 25 November 1845 – an incredible feat by contractor and workmen alike. Vernon Scott has quoted official records as saying:

The Defensible Barracks were built high up on the top of what quickly became known as the Barrack Hill. A huge set of buildings, the barracks occupy an area of 6000 yards and are said to have been built in just one year. If true, it was an incredible feat of engineering.

Possession was taken at three o'clock in the afternoon and was officially indicated by the hoisting of Her Majesty's flag amidst deafening cheers from hundreds of spectators. A substantial dinner with a liberal quantity of double strength Welsh ale was given to the workmen.

Given the speed of the construction process there is no doubt that the workers enjoyed and deserved their treat!

The new barracks occupied an area of 6000 square yards and were originally to have been called The Prince Albert Barracks, in honour of the Queen's husband. This plan was soon dropped and the name Defensible Barracks employed instead. As soon as the barracks were ready the Royal Marines transferred from the *Dragon*, the old ship having become highly inflammable due to the annual coating of pitch and tar needed to keep her watertight. She was duly broken up in 1850. The joy of the Marines at being accommodated in cosy, purpose-built barracks can only be imagined – even if they did have further to walk for their off-duty pint of beer.

For many years the deep moat surrounding the barracks was not fenced in. Several soldiers, returning from a night in one of the town's many hostelries, fell into the open moat and were killed or injured. In particular, two victims of this unmarked hazard have gone down in Pembroke Dock folklore. The first was a certain Dr Sumpter, a local GP. He fell into the moat when returning from a visit to a patient in Pennar one dark night and subsequently died from shock to his nervous system and from his physical injuries.

The other renowned victim was Private John Harding of the Royal Marines. He pitched head first into the moat on 10 October 1850. Harding was duly buried in the town cemetery in Park Street, his headstone reading:

> Except the Lord direct our feet,
> And guide with gracious care;
> At every step we danger meet,
> In every path a snare.
>
> Then reader pause, who e'er thou art,
> As thus my grave you view;
> Remember, thou from life must part,
> Perhaps as quickly, too.

Considering how the unfortunate Harding met his end, the author of the verse must have had his tongue pressed very firmly into his cheek.

During the Crimean War a hut encampment was built at Llanion on land overlooking the Haven. It was intended to house the overflow of soldiers from the Defensible Barracks.

In 1906 the wooden buildings of the Hut Encampment were replaced by a purpose-built set of barracks. This state of the art facility was one of the first military buildings in the country to provide soldiers with separate living, sleeping and dining areas.

The original occupants of the Defensible Barracks were, in time, replaced by men from various regiments, units such as the 11th Foot and the 8th Depot Regiment, as the significance of the dockyard continued to grow. The barracks were undoubtedly a remarkable creation, a government report on the state of the dockyard in 1843 commenting:

> On the hill to the south of the yard and town a 'defensible barrack' is nearing completion and will contain 400 men. It is a perfect work of its kind, and there is not another like it in Great Britain.

During the Crimean War a Hut Encampment was built on land owned by the military at Llanion, overlooking the Hobbs Point Jetty. It was originally intended to take the overflow of troops from the Defensible Barracks but, in the event, proved so useful that by 1904 the wooden huts had been demolished and construction begun on a purpose-built set of barracks in their place. The old huts had been condemned by Field Marshal His Royal Highness the Duke of Cambridge, in 1894 but the new barrack blocks were considered to be the height of modern technology. They were some of the first military buildings in the country to offer soldiers separate facilities for eating and sleeping.

The Crimean War saw a great deal of military activity in Pembroke Dock. By now the place had become a military centre of some significance and with Britain involved in a serious conflict for the first time in forty years, large numbers of troops were mustered in the town. The story of the Crimean War is well known. Suffice it to say that the campaign was run by old men who had not seen action before or, if they had, it was so long ago that the experience was totally invalid and worthless. Lord Raglan, the Commander in Chief, actually thought he was fighting the French – his allies – rather than the Russians. Small wonder, then, that the war was a series of military blunders that were unsurpassed in British military history. Many of the men who left Pembroke Dock did not return to their native shores, most of them dying in the foul and filthy dens that passed as hospitals during the campaign.

The men of the 31st East Surrey Regiment were encamped on the Barrack Hill as there was no room in the barracks themselves. They

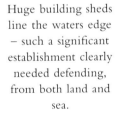

Huge building sheds line the waters edge – such a significant establishment clearly needed defending, from both land and sea.

received their embarkation orders on 6th February 1855 and, a few weeks later, assembled on the parade ground of the barracks, ready to march down to the dockyard and the troopship *Imperadore* that lay waiting for them. According to Mrs Peters:

> The ground on that morning was covered with a sprinkling of snow and the air was bitterly cold and cheerless. The soldiers marched from the Hill to the dockyard steps amidst much excitement and many tokens of grief from wives, families and friends, who accompanied them in order to bid them farewell as they embarked on the *Imperadore* for the East.

Mrs Peters was undoubtedly being discreet. Most of the soldiers had said their farewells the night before, in the smoke-filled taverns of Pembroke and Pembroke Dock. Like all departing regiments the soldiers would have experienced a mixture of fond farewells, recriminations, sexual liaisons and much drinking of beer. The officers had already held a 'farewell ball', to which all the gentry of the area had been invited, altogether a more refined occasion.

The famous Victorian hero Charles Gordon, 'Gordon of Khartoum' as he was to become, was serving in the Royal Engineers and was in Pembroke Dock at this time. He lodged in a house at the conjunction of Bush Street and Lewis Street and was a familiar figure in the town, often to be seen reading a book and walking about on the lower margins of the Barrack Hill. When he received his orders to depart for the war Gordon is said to have announced 'I have received my death warrant!' He left the town with the 31st East Surreys on board the *Imperadore* and, while he lived for several years longer before finally meeting his end in the siege of Khartoum, he never saw Pembroke Dock or the Haven again.

Many famous regiments served in Pembroke Dock in the years after 1855. Amongst them were the Monmouthshire Light Infantry, the Gloucestershire Regiment and the Antrim Militia. However, many militia regiments were garrisoned in Pembroke Dock during the Crimean War as regular army forces were serving in the Crimea. The newcomers, apparently, quickly enlivened the town – not an easy thing to do in a community well used to hard-drinking dockyard workers – as they were a rather hardened class of men, much given to practical jokes and noisy evenings on the town.

At one stage over a hundred members of the Monmouthshire Militia, then stationed in the town, demanded their discharge under the terms of the Militia Act. They refused to go on duty, leaving the dockyard unde-fended, and headed off for the town's pubs and brothels. As Keith Johnson has written:

> When a military picket arrived outside the Duke of Wellington in search of some of the men who had gone AWOL, licensee Kent refused to admit them. He told a Royal Artillery Lieutenant: 'If I was a private I would shoot you. I might shoot you anyway if you don't take care.'

As there were more militiamen than the Defensible Barracks could accommodate, many of this 'rough and licentious soldiery' had to be billeted on the people of the town. The locals were undoubtedly very happy when the militia regiments left and regular army units replaced them once more.

The Gloucestershire Regiment, then known as the Royal North Gloucestershire Regiment, were, together with the Monmouthshire Militia, the first unit to occupy the new Hut Encampment at Llanion. Situated high on the hill, overlooking the river and Haven, the crude wooden huts cannot have been the height of luxury but at least they were more welcome than tents, which would have been the only alternative for the soldiers.

After the Crimean War, in the early 1860s, the crack 15th Brigade, an elite corps of battle-hardened veterans, was posted to the Defensible Barracks. When they left after their tour of duty they did so with muffled drums due to the death of Prince Albert, the Queen's husband and Prince Consort. The regiment was succeeded by the noted 62nd Wiltshire Regiment. Within months of their arrival the regimental band had played during the ceremony to unveil a statue commemorating Prince Albert on Castle Hill in Tenby.

Defending the dockyard was always uppermost in the minds of naval and military planners, particularly in the period immediately following the momentous year of 1848. That was the 'Year of Revolutions' in Europe, the French monarchy toppling for the second time in a hundred years and chaos being brought to countries such as Italy and the Germanic states. Viscount Palmerston and his government soon realised that most of Britain's dockyards were highly vulnerable to attack from the sea. Pembroke Dockyard was no different from the rest. Forts like the Defensible Barracks and the Hut Encampment were places to hold large quantities of soldiers but, if the yards were to be properly protected, then heavy artillery would be required. The memory of the abortive French raid on Fishguard in 1797 remained strong. Nobody could forget how easily the French had obtained a foothold. A few forts, complete with modern cannon, would have made all the difference and while the relative isolation of Pembroke Dock was, in some respects, a strength, it could also be a decided drawback.

Clearly forts – a whole series of them – were required if the yards were going to be made totally safe. When the planners had finished their work, 13 forts of one type or another had been built along the Milford Haven waterway. These included one on Stack Rock, in the middle of the estuary. This self-contained fort was completed by 1850 while another similar defence work was built on Thorne Island at West Angle Bay in 1852. Dale Fort and West Blockhouse Fort were completed later in the century.

When the forts were finished and in place they would have presented any attacking force with a considerable challenge as it attempted to sail up the Haven towards the dockyard. Readers of CS Forrester's *Hornblower* novels will remember that when it came to a contest between wooden warships and land based artillery, the heavy guns of the protected forts invariably came off best! It was a lesson well learned by the defenders of Pembroke Dock and its dockyard.

In the end the forts were never put to use. War with France was avoided and the forts – right across Britain – quickly became known as Palmerston Follies, mainly because the threat of war had come and gone before they had ever finished building them. Most of them sat waiting – many of them are still waiting – for the invader who never came. They remain a powerful symbol of the time, even though they were, in the main, obsolete and old-fashioned long before they were commissioned.

Closer to the dockyard at Pembroke Dock, a heavy concentration of fire power had been built up. Following the dismantling of the old fort at Paterchurch Point, the Admiralty replaced it with the Pater Battery. This was built between 1840 and 1842, and renovated after it had been taken over by the Ordnance in 1855. This was done to plans drawn up by Lieutenant Gordon, as he then was. The Battery mounted no fewer than 23 heavy guns, among them a breech-loading Armstrong 112 pounder. The Battery was eventually dismantled in 1903, having then become obsolete.

In addition to the Pater Battery, two large gun towers were built at the south-western and north-eastern corners of the dockyard. Sometimes mistakenly referred to as Martello Towers, these powerful forts were constructed between 1848 and 1851 by Charles Rigby & Sons. They

Between 1849 and 1857 two huge gun towers – sometimes mistakenly called Martello Towers – were built close to the dockyard. This view shows the western tower and, beyond it, the remains of the Pater Battery which housed the original artillery defence for the yards. Pater Battery was demolished in 1903.

were designed to house one officer and thirty-three artillerymen. The gunners would have manned the three 32 pounder smooth bore cannon that formed the main battery for the towers. These guns would have been mounted on the roof of the tower. There were also three 12 pounder bronze howitzers on the main level of the fort while each soldier would also have been issued with a muzzle-loading carbine.

By the late 1870s the rapid development of armoured warships and rifled guns that fired high explosive shells meant that the smooth bore weapons in the two gun towers were obsolete. The weapons had been removed by 1882 and, in light of the other defensive forts on the waterway, the towers were never rearmed. In many respects they were like the gunboats of Victoria's navy, too weak to fight, too slow to run away. In the case of the Pembroke Dock gun towers they were too small, and too vulnerable to attack from the sea.

In the years leading up to the end of the nineteenth century dozens of famous regiments served at Pembroke Dock. These included the 1st Battalion Royal Welch Fusiliers, the 9th East Norfolks (known as the 'Holy Boys') and the 36th Worcestershires. This regiment was the last unit stationed at Pembroke Dock to wear the old fashioned shako and have green facings on their uniforms.

The north-east gun tower is shown in this postcard from the turn of the nineteenth century.

In the 1880s the 81st Loyal North Lancashire Regiment arrived for a tour of duty in the town. As Vernon Scott has noted, in *PD Days*:

Their stay is of some interest because during this time the garrison chaplain, the Rev. Stuart Patterson, discovered in the regiment's possessions a Bible on which 'the first President of the United States, George Washington, took his Freemasonry Oath.' This must have been a relic of the American War of Independence in which the North Lancs had fought a century before.

Being a military and dockyard town, marches and parades were a common feature of life in Pembroke Dock. This pre-1914 photograph shows dockyard officials in their distinctive cocked hats marching alongside soldiers, policemen and several excited children.

Other regiments to serve at Pembroke Dock included the 88th Connaught Rangers and the 2nd Battalion of the 24th South Wales Borderers. Famed as the regiment of Rorke's Drift, where they won more Victoria Crosses in a single action than any other regiment in the British army, the South Wales Borderers marched to Pembroke Dock from their base in Brecon. The Regiment paused for a rest at Pembroke Castle where they were given refreshments and officially welcomed by the Mayor of the Borough, Councillor Samuel J. Allen. The Mayor and members of the Corporation then travelled to the Defensible Barracks in front of the Borderers in a four-horse break while cheering crowds thronged the streets and roadways.

When the Boer War broke out it was like a repetition of the Crimean War. In 1855 it had been the East Surreys who had marched gallantly and eagerly off to war, now it was the men of the 1st Battalion Royal Welch Fusiliers. On Sunday 22 October, with band playing and flags flying, the regiment marched to the railway station in the town and entrained for Southampton, *en route* to Durban and action in the latest war on behalf of the British Empire.

On the very day of departure there was a fatal accident when Drummer Grainger of the Fusiliers accidentally discharged his rifle. The bullet passed

Another parade, this view was taken by the town's major photographer, S. J. Allen, from the upstairs window of his shop and studio in Bush Street.

through the wall of the hut and hit a reservist by the name of Jones, killing him instantly. Grainger was fortunate. Arrested and detained while an Inquiry was held, he missed the boat to South Africa. Subsequently found to be innocent, he also missed the carnage of the Boer War where, amongst other casualties in the regiment, the commanding officer, Colonel Thorold, was shot and killed.

About 1899 married quarters for artillerymen were built on the eastern rim of the Barrack Hill, some old cottages being pulled down to make way for the new buildings. At more or less the same time the Royal Engineers Barracks at Pennar were completed, the land having been given to the military as far back as 1830. Submarine mining experiments had been carried on for some time in the area, on the shore of Pennar Gut, a total sum of £17,000 having been spent in establishing the Engineers Barracks and the mining works. It was the third major barracks block in the town.

In the run up to the Great War, regiments continued to come and go at Pembroke Dock. Llanion, once the new purpose-built huts became operational in 1904, soon superseded the Defensible Barracks as the town's main quarters for soldiers. The Defensible Barracks had served the country and the town well but, by the turn of the nineteenth century, were too

Yet another parade, this time showing soldiers coming down into the town from the barracks at Llanion.

old and ill-equipped to offer the services that modern soldiering required. Despite this, the barracks continued to be used for small groups of soldiers, regulars and territorials alike, until the mid-1950s.

Before long Llanion Barracks included a new hospital, a garrison prison and a gymnasium. Married quarters were built next, along with a library and a canteen – a far cry, indeed, from the days when the first Royal Marines were billeted on the old and leaking wooden warship *Dragon*.

To the east of the barrack block a military cemetery was created. Many soldiers were laid to rest in this quiet spot, some of them being casualties brought back to Wales from the Western Front during the Great War. The largest funeral ever to take place in the cemetery, however, was apparently that of Colonel Isaac Moore of the 13th Depot Battalion who was buried there on 14 October 1868.

Hundreds of eager Pembrokeshire recruits enlisted for service at Llanion Barracks during the Great War, all eager to 'do their bit' for King and Country, all fearful that the war would be over by Christmas, before they could get out to France. They need not have worried. The killing machine of the Western Front would take all the men that Britain could give and it would be four long years before peace was restored to the world.

Once the war ended the renowned and famous regiments began to

A military funeral moves down Bush Street in the town.

return to Pembroke Dock, most of them for a traditional two or three year stint of duty. Between 1918 and the beginning of the Second World War units like the Royal Welch Fusiliers, the King's Shropshire Light Infantry and the East Lancs were based at Llanion Barracks. When Chamberlain made his ominous and historic broadcast to the British nation on Sunday, 3 September 1939 it was the Buffs who formed the town's garrison.

In October 1943 men of the American 110th Infantry Regiment were posted to Llanion Barracks. Route marches in the Preseli Mountains and amphibious exercises on the county's beaches were the order of the day for the young American soldiers. On 1 April 1944 General Dwight Eisenhower, the Supreme Allied Commander, paid a sudden and surprise visit to the 110th Regiment. He arrived by train at Tenby and was then taken in a fast convoy, complete with motor cycle out-riders, to the HQ of the 110th at Llanion Barracks.

The military cemetery at Llanion.

Despite chilly, damp weather, Ike climbed into the back of a jeep and spoke to the men, promising to have a drink with them on the day that the unit crossed the Rhine. He then visited outlying units of the regiment before driving back to his headquarters.

The 110th remained in occupation at Llanion, with small companies stationed at places like Lamphey, Cresselly and Haverfordwest, until April 1944 when, under the cover of darkness, the 5000 strong force left Pembroke Dock to prepare for the D-Day landings. Sadly, the regiment suffered particularly heavy casualties during the Normandy invasion and in subsequent campaigns like the Battle of the Bulge. The 110th was replaced at Llanion Barracks by the 2nd US Infantry Division but their stay was very brief before they too left Pembroke Dock for duties in Europe.

Despite their relatively short stay, the GIs were popular with the locals, in particular with the unattached ladies of the town and young school children. The cry of 'Got any gum, chum?' was undoubtedly often heard on the streets of Pembroke Dock during these years.

After the end of hostilities in 1945, British troops returned to Llanion Barracks for garrison duties. For the people of Pembroke Dock it was simply a case of 'business as usual'. In the mid 1950s, when the 1st Battalion Welch Regiment arrived in Pembroke Dock there was a huge outpouring of affection from the people of the town, dozens of locals gathering along the streets to cheer and wave as the Regiment marched past. They were succeeded by the 22nd Light Anti-Aircraft Regiment, a unit that soon had a local café and dance hall named after it – the renowned 'Double Two' on London Road, a place where soldiers and locals alike used to gather to dance and gossip in the evenings.

Llanion Barracks finally became surplus to military requirements in 1966. The Royal Engineers Barracks at Pennar were de-commissioned at about the same time, and, of course, the old Defensible Barracks had already closed their doors to troops. In 1974 Llanion Barracks became the headquarters of the newly formed South Pembrokeshire District Council, a rôle they filled until the early years of the twenty-first century, while the Pennar Barracks became, for a while, a holiday complex and dance hall. Llanion is now home to the headquarters of the Pembrokeshire Park Authority, much of the land and barrack block space having been turned over to private housing. The Pennar Barracks have been demolished and new houses built on the site.

The Royal Engineers Barracks at Pennar were built in conjunction with a submarine mining depot in 1875.

Pembroke Dock. Pennar Barracks.

A classic view of the Haven and dockyard, taken from the hut encampment, with a County Class cruiser sitting alongside Hobbs Point.

Pembroke Dock from Huts.

The Defensible Barracks, the huge monolith that still dominates the town, are now empty, despite having once been home to the South Pembs Golf Club. For several years they also housed a works depot and stores for the South Pembrokeshire District Council. There have been talks and plans to convert them into a hotel but such schemes have come to nothing. Perhaps in the future...

When the military departed it was undoubtedly a sad day for the people of Pembroke Dock. The place had always been a soldiers' town. They were regularly seen in the shops and pubs or marching in parades through the wide streets. It had always been a military town, much more than a naval one. Sailors were rarely seen in the place, ships being launched and sailing away, returning only rarely. Apart from Guard Ships such as HMS *Blenheim*, used as a base for Royal Marines between April 1862 and April 1864, no warships were stationed at the port. Pembroke Dock was a dockyard town, not a naval one.

In reality the town always had far stronger connections with the army and, in the years after 1930, with the RAF than it ever had with the 'Senior Service'. The dockyard closed in 1926 but the military remained in the town for another forty years! And yet, in popular mythology, it is as a naval centre that the place is remembered. The fact is, nothing could be further from the truth.

CHAPTER FIVE

The Ships

I N A P E R I O D O F just over 100 years the ships of Pembroke Dockyard, from the *Ariadne* and *Valorous* of 1814 to the final dockyard vessel, the *Oleander*, launched in 1922, were renowned, not only for their quality but also for the position that many of them held in naval history.

Launches were usually carried out at High Water Spring and Autumn tides, the relatively shallow water around the dockyard being taken into consideration, even in the early days. Only in the case of very small vessels was it possible to launch two ships on the same tide. This meant that, when ships had been built together, there invariably had to be a second launch, almost exactly one calendar month after the first. Despite this obvious drawback, Pembroke Dockyard quickly established itself as a powerful force. In 1816 it was the only dockyard in the country to be expanding

Launches were always popular and well attended, by local dignitaries and working people alike.

and the ships that soon began to take shape on its slipways became famous names in British naval history.

The first ship ever launched from the yards was the 28-gun sixth-rate *Ariadne*. She slipped into the water bow first on 10 February 1816, followed shortly afterwards by her sister ship, this time stern first off the same building slip. The *Ariadne* was destined to be the last sea-going command of Captain Frederick Marryat. Having joined the navy in 1806, Marryat just missed the Battle of Trafalgar but served throughout the final stages of the campaign against Napoleon. During an adventurous and action-filled career, Marryat won The Royal Humane Society's Gold Medal for Bravery. However, it is for his children's novels, clearly based on his own experiences, that Marryat is best remembered, the adventure tales *Mr Midshipman Easy* and *Masterman Ready* being the most famous. He took command of the *Ariadne* on 10 November 1828.

It is interesting to ponder which of his characters and plots came into Marryat's head as he paced the quarterdeck of the old frigate or even whether he ever sailed her into the Haven where she was built. What is known is that his second novel, *The Kings Own*, was completed on board the *Ariadne*, presumably while her commander was waiting to be discharged from the navy.

The *Hamadryad* was the eighteenth vessel to be launched from the

Hundreds of famous ships were launched from the yards, none more renowned than the *Hamadryad* of 1823 which finished her days as a hospital ship in Cardiff docks.

dockyard on 25 July 1823, costing the incredible sum of £24,683. The 46-gun frigate was destined never to see action and was actually laid up at Devonport, ready for breaking, when it was decided that she should be converted into the Seaman's Hospital Ship at Cardiff. At that time the great coal port was desperately in need of hospital facilities as ships were beginning to pour into the docks from all over the world. The *Hamadryad* was duly towed to Cardiff and moored in the docks. She commenced her duties on 1 November 1866 and served until 1905, catering for over 170,000 patients from every corner of the globe. Although the old ship has now gone, her name remains. The Hamadryad Hospital still operates in the docks area of Cardiff.

On 2 April 1833 the *Royal William* was launched amidst great celebration and glee from dockyard workers and thousands of spectators who had flocked to view the event. The *Royal William* was Pembroke Dockyard's first vessel to carry over 100 guns and, therefore, her launch was a matter of some significance in the town. The dockyard had already produced many large ships, the 84-gun *Clarence* – after which one of the town's premier inns was named – and the *Belleisle* of 74 guns being just two. The creation of the *Royal William*, however, marked an important stage in the development of the yards.

The covered building sheds of the dockyard are clearly shown in this cabinet photograph that dates from about 1860.

Interestingly, the *Royal William*, like the *Hamadryad*, went on to another career once her naval days were over. She was re-christened *Clarence* and taken to the Mersey where she replaced a previous *Clarence* – also built at Pembroke Dockyard – as a training ship for the Liverpool Catholic Reformatory Society. The first *Clarence* had come to an untimely end when she was burned to the waterline by the inmates who clearly did not relish the prospect of a career at sea. The *Royal William*, now *Clarence II* met a similar fate, again due to arson, in July 1899, a sad end for a once-proud ship.

The wooden paddle frigate *Cyclops* slipped into the waters of the Haven on 10 July 1839. She had originally been rated as a steam sloop but her displacement of 1960 tons caused her to be re-rated as a frigate. Together with her sister ship *Gorgon*, the *Cyclops* was the Royal Navy's first steam vessel of over 1000 tons. In a distinguished career she served in the Syrian Campaign of 1840 – one of Britain's early Empire wars – and in the Black Sea during the Crimean War. She then helped to lay the first transatlantic telegraph cable, in 1857.

By 1843 the dockyard was well established. A report commissioned by the Admiralty that year commented:

> Although this naval establishment in Wales is not a port where ships are generally commissioned and fitted out, and therefore does not attract as much notice as other establishments around the United Kingdom, it is not without considerable importance, and as a ship building yard is, perhaps, superior to most of the others.

This shot of the dockyard and the Haven shows an early ironclad moored off Hobbs Point. Carr Jetty is not shown so that dates the view to approximately 1880.

The writer of the report had put his finger quite neatly on the major problem of Pembroke Dockyard. It was not a fitting-out yard. Once ships were launched they would be hastily fitted with a jury rig and sailed around the coast to Devonport or Portsmouth where they would be completed. Louisa M. Sabine Pasley, daughter of one-time Captain Superintendent Sir Thomas Sabine Pasley, wrote about the period 1849–1854 when she lived in the town with her father:

> Ships seemed to have been turned off by the dozen in those days. No sooner was the launch over than round came a party of riggers from Devonport, the ship had her masts and yards in ... and the interest was concentrated on some other vessel.

Pembroke Dockyard did not become a fitting-out base until the latter years of the nineteenth century when Hobbs Point was converted for the process and a huge set of sheer legs, capable of lifting the heaviest boilers, was built on the jetty. Like giant barbers' poles the legs reached up into the sky, dominating the lower regions of the town as surely as the Defensible Barracks dominated the upper portion.

It was, at best, a stop-gap provision, ships having to be towed across from the dockyard to Hobbs Point once they had been launched. The fact that gigantic vessels like the *Renown* and *Hannibal* could be provided with engines alongside such a tiny berth or jetty speaks volumes for the quality of the Pembroke Dock workforce. Not until the end of the century did full fitting-out services arrive with the armoured cruiser HMS *Essex* being the first vessel to be entirely fitted out at Pembroke Dockyard. That was as late in the history of the yards as 1901.

At the end of the 1840s Pembroke Dockyard had twelve building slips, most of them covered over. The reason for the large number of slips is simply that the construction process demanded it. Timber for the ships frames was soaked in the dockyard's 'pickling pond' before being taken to the kilns where they were steamed and worked into the correct shape. They were then used in the building process and the partially completed ship was left to 'season' on the slip. It meant that ships could be left on the stocks for long periods of time, without any risk of damage. The *Windsor Castle*, eventually launched in 1858, for example, stood on the slipway for nearly fourteen years.

The 1843 Report into the state of the dockyard seems to catch, exactly, the mood of the place and the style of building involved:

> Slips 1 and 2 are presently vacant and have no roofs over them. On slip

3 the frame of the Lion, 80 guns, is now complete. On slip 4 is more than half of the frame for the Victoria, 110 guns; but the building has been stopped by order of the Admiralty dated the 18th December last. On slip 5 the 50 gun frigate *Constance* is about three-eighths completed. On slip 6 is laid the Colossus, with frame completed. On slip 7 the steam frigate Dragon is being built, and is half completed. All the above slips are fit for building first-rates.

Slips 8 and 9 are vacant; they are fit for two-deck line of battle ships. On slip 10 the 36 gun Sybille is about three-eighths completed. On slip 11 the Inflexible steam sloop is laid down, and is half built. On slip 12 the brig Kingfisher is about five-eighths advanced.

Clearly, then, the place was a hive of activity; within the previous twelve months a further 14 acres had been added to the total acreage of the establishment. There was a downside to this process of construction, however. The yards had been established not long after Nelson's victory at Trafalgar, when ship design and styles of building had changed very little for hundreds of years. In a time of rapid technological change and advance, such as to be found in the mid-nineteenth century, there was a very real danger that ships built 'the Pembroke Dock way' could be obsolete even before completion. In some respects, then, the demise of Pembroke Dockyard can be seen as early as twenty years after it came into existence.

H. M. S. ESSEX AT HOBBS POINT

HMS *Essex* alongside the fitting-out berth of Hobbs Point.

LAUNCH OF HER MAJESTY'S NEW YACHT, "THE VICTORIA AND ALBERT," AT THE ROYAL DOCKYARD, PEMBROKE.

The yards at Pembroke Dock built four Royal Yachts as well as a Passage Boat for Queen Victoria. This print shows the launch of the paddle yacht *Victoria and Albert* in 1855.

For the moment, however, the yards continued to turn out vessels of great beauty and power. On 26 April 1843 Pembroke Dock built its first Royal Yacht, the paddler *Victoria and Albert*. The workmen were conscious of the honour bestowed upon them and the dockyard by the commission to build the yacht – it was an honour that was to be repeated when a replacement vessel was launched on 16 January 1855. She was originally to have been called *Windsor Castle* but, eventually, was christened with the same name as the Queen's first yacht, *Victoria and Albert*. Lord Milford performed the naming ceremony, just as Lady Cawdor had named the first one.

Ultimately, the yards at Pembroke Dock built four Royal Yachts – the two 'V & A's mentioned above, the *Osborne* (built for the Prince of Wales in December 1870) and a third *Victoria and Albert*, launched on 9 May 1899. The stability of this last named vessel was thought by many of the dockyard workmen to be faulty – an opinion shared by the Queen herself, who did not like the design of the ship and made her opinions well known. As if to confirm these feelings the Royal Yacht actually keeled over when the dry dock, in which she had been completed, was flooded with water in order to float her out.

The *Victoria and Albert* had been moved from Hobbs Point as the cruiser *Spartiate* needed to be fitted out and no other jetty was available. Prompt

action by the dockyard staff ensured there was only minimal damage and the next day, 4 January 1900, she was taken out to a buoy where her stability was tested. Over 400 men were used to rush from side to side of the new yacht and the effect measured. An enquiry subsequently found that the vessel was top-heavy, due to an excess in weight and equipment. Sir William White, designer of the new yacht and the Director of Naval Construction, felt obliged to hand in his resignation and retired, a broken man.

In addition to the four Royal Yachts, the yards at Pembroke Dock also built the *Alberta*, a passage boat for the Queen. She was launched on 3 October 1863 and, together with the *Osborne*, became the Queen's favourite yacht. It was the *Alberta* that carried Victoria's body from Osborne on the Isle of Wight to Portsmouth on 1 February 1901.

In 1851 the yards produced the last paddle frigate ever built for the Royal Navy, HMS *Valorous*. A few years later, on the evening of 21 October 1860, came the enormous line of battle ship *Howe*, the last three-decker built for the Royal Navy. Twice the size of Nelson's *Victory*, she had a displacement of 6,577 tons, one of the largest wooden steam battleships ever built.

On 14 September 1852 a wooden three-decked warship was launched from the yards. She was to be called the *Windsor Castle* but, on the day of her launch, news was received of the death of the Duke of Wellington, victor of Waterloo and subsequently prime minister of the country. A few days later the Admiralty decided, in honour of the Duke, that the ship's name should be changed to *Duke of Wellington*.

Originally named *Windsor Castle*, this print shows the launch of the largest wooden battleship ever built, the *Duke of Wellington*. The ship was renamed following the news of the death of the great Iron Duke, victor at Waterloo and later prime minister of Britain.

A mammoth vessel, the *Duke of Wellington* was remarkable for the fact that mid-way through her construction it was decided to extend her length. The hull was cut into two separate parts and the rear section launched out into the Haven. It was then carefully positioned 23 feet away from the front half and a new middle section built to join the two halves. It was all done in order to provide extra displacement for engines and boilers. The *Duke of Wellington*, the largest wooden battleship ever built, was also the first large vessel to be fitted with a screw propeller. According to W. P. Trotter:

> It is on record that to build HMS *Duke of Wellington* – 250 feet long with a beam of 60 feet – an oak forest of seventy-six acres was cleared of trees.

The giant ship was the flag ship of Admiral Napier during the Crimean War, led the Naval Review at Spithead in 1855 and finished her days as a Depot Ship in Portsmouth Dockyard.

Launchings at Pembroke Dock were always grand affairs. The dockyard gates would be swung open and from early morning spectators would flock inside to stand and watch in awe. Many of them brought picnics and spent

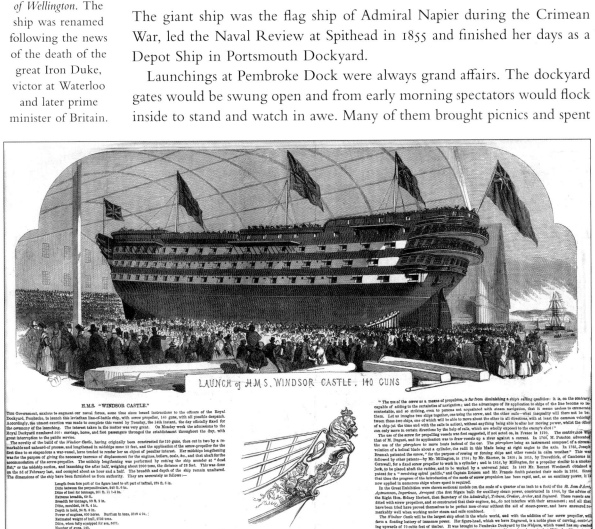

LAUNCH of H.M.S. WINDSOR CASTLE, 140 GUNS

H.M.S. "WINDSOR CASTLE."

THE Government, anxious to augment our naval forces, some time since issued instructions to the officers of the Royal Dockyard, Pembroke, to launch this leviathan line-of-battle ship, with screw propeller, 140 guns, with all possible despatch. Accordingly, the utmost exertion was made to complete this vessel by Tuesday, the 14th instant, the day officially fixed for the ceremony of the launching. The interest taken in the matter was very great. On Monday week the admissions to the Royal Dockyard numbered 500 : carriage, horse, and foot passengers thronged the establishment throughout the day, with great interruption to the public service.

The novelty of the build of the *Windsor Castle*, having originally been constructed for 120 guns, then cut in two by a remarkable and unheard-of process, and lengthened in midships some 23 feet, and the application of the screw-propeller for the first time to so stupendous a war-vessel, have tended to render her an object of peculiar interest. Her midships lengthening was for the purpose of giving the necessary increase of displacement for the engines, boilers, coals, &c., and that shaft for the accommodation of the screw-propeller. The midship lengthening was performed by cutting the ship asunder at "dead flat," or the midship section, and launching the after half, weighing about 2000 tons, the distance of 23 feet. This was done on the 3d of February last, and occupied an hour and a half. The breadth and depth of the ship remain unaltered. The dimensions of the ship have been furnished us from authority. They are accurately as follows :—

Length from fore part of the figure head to aft part of taffrail, 278 ft. 6 in.
Ditto between the perpendiculars, 240 ft. 6 in.
Ditto of keel for tonnage, 201 ft. 11 1-3 in.
Extreme breadth, 60 ft.
Breadth for tonnage, 59 ft. 2 in.
Ditto, moulded, 58 ft. 4 in.
Depth in hold, 24 ft. 8 in.
Power of engines, 800 horse. Burthen in tons, 3759 4 94.
Estimated weight of hull, 3732 tons.
Ditto, when fully equipped for sea, 5571.
Number of guns, 140.

The comparative advantage of screw propulsion, as applied to this leviathan vessel, are thus explained in an admirable report by Lieutenant Labrousse, of the French navy :—

FIGURE-HEAD OF THE "WINDSOR CASTLE."

" The use of the screw as a means of propulsion, is far from diminishing a ship's sailing qualities: it is, on the contrary, capable of adding to the certainties of navigation ; and the advantages of its application to ships of the line become so incontestable, and so striking, even to persons not acquainted with steam navigation, that it seems useless to enumerate them. Let us imagine two ships close together, one using the screw, and the other sails—what inequality will there not be between these two ships, one of which will be able to move about the other in all directions, with at least the common velocity of a ship (at the time and with the sails in action), without anything being able to alter her moving power, whilst the other can only move in certain directions by the help of sails, which are wholly exposed to the enemy's shot !"

The use of the screw for propelling vessels was first suggested, if not acted on, in France in 1720. The contrivance was that of M. Duquet, and its application was to draw vessels up a river against a current. In 1768, M. Punction advocated the use of the *œtrophore* to move boats instead of the oar. The *œtrophore* being an instrument composed of a circumvolution of a helical blade about a cylinder, the radii in this blade being at right angles to the axis. In 1785, Joseph Bramah patented the screw, " for the purpose of rowing or forcing ships and other vessels in calm weather." This was followed by other patents—by Mr. Millington, in 1794 ; by Mr. Shorter, in 1800 ; in 1815, by Trevethick, of Camborne in Cornwall, for a fixed screw propeller to work in a cylinder ; and in 1816, by Millington, for a propeller similar to a smoke-Jack, to be placed abaft the rudder, and to be worked by a universal joint. In 1832 Mr. Bennet Woodcroft obtained a patent for a " revolving spiral paddle," and Captain Ericsson and Mr. Francis Smith patented their mode in 1836. Since that time the progress of the introduction of the mode of screw propulsion has been rapid, and, as an auxiliary power, it is now applied in numerous ships where speed is required.

In the Great Exhibition were shown sectional models (on the scale of a quarter of an inch to a foot) of the *St. Jean d'Acre*, *Agamemnon*, *Imperieuse*, *Arrogant* (the first frigate built for auxiliary steam power, constructed in 1844, by the advice of the Right Hon. Sidney Herbert, then Secretary of the Admiralty), *Tribune*, *Cruiser*, *Archer*, and *Reynard*. These vessels are fitted with screw propellers, and so constructed that their engines, &c., do not interfere with their armament ; and all that have been tried have proved themselves to be perfect men-of-war without the aid of steam-power, and have answered remarkably well when working under steam and sails combined.

The *Windsor Castle* will be the largest ship afloat in the whole world, and with the addition of her screw propeller, will form a floating battery of immense power. Her figure-head, which we have Engraved, is a noble piece of carving, containing upwards of 70 cubic feet of timber. It was brought to Pembroke Dockyard by the *Widgeon*, which vessel has superseded the *Prospero*, a steam-tug, tender to *Saturn* guard-ship. H.M. steam-frigate *Simoom* has also arrived at Milford, with masts and rigging for the *Windsor Castle*.

the whole day in the yards, wandering around the slipways and cheering when the ship finally entered the Milford Haven waterway. The official part of the launching ceremony was usually carried out by some dignitary or other. Sometimes these were local people like Lady Milford or Lady Balfour, daughter of the Earl of Cawdor, on other occasions by people like the Duke of Clarence or, when the last *Victoria and Albert* entered the water, by the daughter-in-law of the Queen, the Duchess of York. When the two tiny gunboats *Tickler* and *Griper* were launched in 1879 they were christened by two little girls, Miss E. Warren, daughter of the Chief Constructor, and Miss Powell, the daughter of the town vicar!

Sometimes, however, things did not quite go according to plan. The *Caesar* was a two-decked wooden screw ship of 90 guns, due to be launched on 21 July 1853. The band played, the speeches were given, but the vessel stuck fast, half way down the slip, and simply refused to move. On investigation it was discovered that somebody with a keen eye to economy had ordered fir wood to be used instead of oak on the launching ways. The fir was far too soft and, as a consequence, the *Caesar* simply

The *Caesar* was a 90-gun battleship launched from the yards in 1853. Rumours of sorcery and witchcraft surrounded her launch.

The launch of the *James Watt* at Pembroke Dockyard, 23 April 1853.

bedded herself into the wood. As if that was not enough, the tallow that was used to grease the ways was of very inferior quality.

As far as the people of Pembroke Dock were concerned, however, the failure of the launch was due to a local woman, a supposed witch called Betty Foggy. Having been turned away from the dockyard gates when she tried to get in and watch the launch, Betty had been heard to mumble 'Very well, then there'll be no launch today!' Her curse seemed to work and it was Sunday 7 August, with the people of the town conveniently at divine service, before the *Caesar* finally slid into the water. For 17 days workmen had been building huge wooden structures, known as camels, under the hull of the stricken ship in order to lift her keel out of the soft fir.

On the occasion of the launch of the two gunboats *Janus* and *Drake* in March 1856, the *Drake* caught on the stocks and smashed into the wooden gantry that had been erected for the visiting dignitaries and officials. Several of them were injured, Mrs Mathias of nearby Lamphey Court

having to be taken to the Dockyard Surgery to be given first aid for her broken collar bone.

As wooden sailing vessels gave way to steam and iron, so the yards at Pembroke Dock adapted to fit in with new technology. Sometimes progress was slow. The *Ajax*, an 8,544-ton iron armour clad, took seven years to complete. Such a delay had been appropriate in the days of wooden warships. Now it was far too long. The *Ajax* was, incidentally, considered to be 'the most unhandy capital ship ever to fly the White Ensign' – not much of an advertisement for the workmanship of Pembroke Dockyard, although, to be fair to the tradesmen in the dockyard, such faults as the vessel possessed were probably due more to poor design than poor construction.

Mostly, though, the workmanship was of a much greater quality. Although, even by this stage, many in the Admiralty had begun to think of Pembroke Dockyard as something of a frontier post – useful but, ultimately, dispensable – the yards continued to grind out ships of superlative quality.

By 1875 Pembroke Dockyard covered almost 80 acres. Nearly 1,500 men were employed there, a figure that was destined to rise to between 2,200

The launch of the *Lord Clyde*, a 24-gun ironclad frigate. The print is from *The Illustrated London News* – launches at Pembroke Dock were always popular with the London press.

and 2,500 by the end of the century. James Anderson Findlay was able to boast that:

> Building sheds rise majestically and barrier-like along the very water's edge. There are joiners, millwrights, blacksmiths, plumbers, copper-smiths, coopers, wheelwrights, painters, pattern-makers and armour plating shops ... near to the docks lie numberless armour plates, varying in thickness from two to eighteen inches, destined to cover the sides of those powerful ships of war, which are being constructed in the neighbouring sheds.

The key to the success of the place was the magnificent warships that seemed to be turned out by the dozen in those halcyon days. The year 1875, about which Findlay was writing, was a relatively quiet one for launches − only two vessels, the armour-plated *Dreadnought* and armour-clad *Shannon* being the only two ships to enter the water. Four years later, however, no fewer than six launches took place. These must have been the ships that Findlay saw being built during his visit.

Several Pembroke Dock ships hold rare distinctions and honours. Along with the Chatham-built *Raleigh*, the *Inconstant* of 1868 was the last Royal Navy warship of the nineteenth century to be officially termed 'frigate' − not until the Second World War was the term revised and used again for convoy escort vessels. The *Inconstant* was, for a time, the fastest ship in the world and was still afloat some eighty-eight years later, the last Pembroke Dock vessel in existence.

The *Edinburgh*, launched on 18 March 1882, was the first Royal Navy battleship to carry a main armament of breech-loading guns and to be fitted with compound rather than iron armour. Huge and lumbering in the water, she was the last of the great Victorian 'citadel' ships. The *Lord*

An early chart of Milford Haven showing the dockyard at Pembroke Dock.

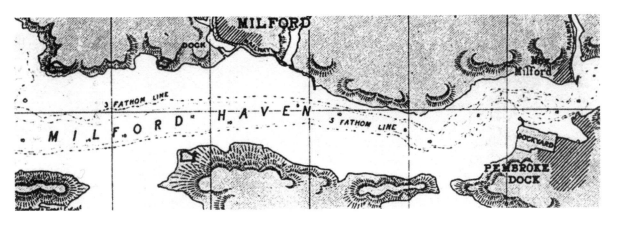

Clive was launched on 13 October 1865 being, along with her sister ship *Lord Warden*, the last true broadside ironclad built for the navy. The *Lord Clyde* was not a successful ship, unseasoned wood having been used in her construction. As a consequence her hull quickly became rotten and, known as 'the Queen's bad bargain', she had come out of service within ten years.

The *Shannon* of 1875 was the first British armoured cruiser while the *Collingwood*, launched in November 1882, was the first British battleship to achieve a speed of 16 knots under steam. She was a vessel which polarised the Admiralty's thinking on battleship style – all succeeding battleship classes, up to the introduction of the *Dreadnought* in 1906 were, really, only improvements and modifications on her design.

The *Renown* (1895) was the first British battleship to be built with an all-steel armour plating while the two

A County Class cruiser, either the *Cornwall* or *Essex*, moored at Hobbs Point for fitting out.

despatch vessels *Iris* and *Mercury* had a significance far beyond their size and purpose. Launched in 1877 and 1878 respectively, they were the first ships in the Royal Navy to be built entirely of steel. Despite their diminutive size, their engines made them the fastest fighting ships in the world.

When the gigantic *Hannibal* slid from the stocks on 28 April 1896 she became the largest vessel ever built at Pembroke Dock. One of the huge Majestic Class of battleships, she seems now to sum up the whole pre-Dreadnought age of warships, representing the very ideal of Victorian power and glory. Her launch was the apogee of Pembroke Dock's career as a ship building centre. The yards continued to build ships, cruisers and submarines in particular, for another thirty years but never again were they to achieve such distinction, never again were they to hold such an important place in the hearts and minds of the Lords of the Admiralty.

Lawrence Phillips has written about the way that Pembroke Dockyard was appreciated at this time:

Even after the opening of the railway through to the dockyard town in August 1864, Pembroke remained a frontier post. 'Pembroke labours under the misfortune of being 300 miles from Whitehall. It is an outpost, and only visited occasionally', commiserated the *United Service Gazette* in 1859, whose writer moreover considered that 'the increasing value and importance of Pembroke as a building yard, seems lost, in great measure on the authorities'.

There is no doubt that the dockyard at Pembroke Dock was, increasingly, forgotten or marginalised as time went on. The yards were usually last in the queue when material and equipment were being handed out and even the long awaited fitting-out berth at Carr Jetty in the years immediately after 1900, built as a supplement to Hobbs Point, were tidal and inadequate when compared to the facilities at other Royal Naval yards. From the closing years of the nineteenth century, then, the writing was on the wall.

The thirteen building slips of Pembroke Dock had made it Britain's principal ship building yard for over a century. Even when iron and steel replaced wood the yards carried on operating, a little tentatively and unsure at times, it has to be admitted, but at least they continued to carry out their essential function and purpose.

By 1855 the town's official Guide Book was proudly boasting that:

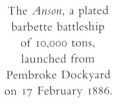

The *Anson*, a plated barbette battleship of 10,000 tons, launched from Pembroke Dockyard on 17 February 1886.

The dockyard is now surrounded by a lofty wall, inclosing [sic] an area of upwards of seventy acres.

The writer went on to describe the range of building slips inside the yards and the huge iron sheds that covered them. These sheds were built by Fox and Henderson, who were also the famous contractors for the Crystal Palace in London. The connection was celebrated by naming one of the nearby pubs The Crystal Palace. At this time the dockyard was employing almost 1000 men and was already the largest 'employment agency' in west Wales.

By the late 1850s the elegant officer's residences along the south wall had been completed, the Captain Superintendent's house, to the left of the main entrance gate, being particularly well appointed. Beyond the houses lay vast piles of timber, brought in from places like the Forest of Dean or Scandinavia, the smell of the wood wafting through the air, assailing the nostrils of everyone who entered the yards. Lining the road from the gate were the solid stone-built offices of the dockyard staff and, beyond these again, lay the building slips and workshops.

Looking back now, with hindsight, it all seems rather brittle, too delicate and finely tuned to survive for long. There was an air of expectation around the town and the dockyard was an undoubted hive of activity but nobody could deny that the establishment was in the wrong place, at the wrong time. As the years went on that drawback only seemed to get worse.

In some respects the tragedy of Pembroke Dock is that its century of ship building saw the greatest and most profound development in naval design that had ever been. Sail gave way to steam, wood to iron and steel. Dockyard workers had to learn how to cope with and understand new technology; they had to acquire strange new skills. Above all they had to learn how to adapt because, in an age of rapid and sudden change, today's skills could suddenly and easily become tomorrow's history.

The story of Pembroke Dock has often been seen as one of promise cut short. In truth, it is a wonder that the dockyard survived for as long as it did.

CHAPTER SIX

Action Stations

PEMBROKE DOCK SHIPS SAW action in many far-flung corners of the world as the British Empire expanded steadily throughout the nineteenth century. Some of them, inevitably, were lost during their service while others went on to achieve immortality and glory. Most of the Pembroke Dock ships were warships, their purpose being to wage war on behalf of the Queen, and in this they seem to have been particularly successful.

The *Vengeance* and *Rodney*, for example, both took part in the first bombardment of the Sebastapol forts on 17 October 1854. The *Rodney* had been launched in June 1833, the first British three-decker to carry over 90 guns. She was towed into action at Sebastapol by another Pembroke Dock vessel, the paddler *Spiteful*, when her enormous broadside was highly effective against the Russian positions.

The last years of the nineteenth century was the time of gunboat diplomacy when the old cliché and standard government response to 'send a gunboat' was a piece of advice that was both appropriate and well used. One small action in which two Pembroke Dock-built gunboats took part serves to show the typical kind of exercise on which ships of this type were constantly engaged.

In 1890 the Portuguese were making moves along the Zambesi, intending to use the river as a route into central Africa. The gunboats *Redbreast* and *Pigeon*, built at Pembroke Dock in 1888 and 1889, crossed the bar at the mouth of the Zambesi, their shallow draughts easing their passage, and then began to force their way upstream. *Pigeon* soon developed engine problems and was forced to return to the open sea but *Redbreast* continued on her way, eventually breaking out into open water. On seeing the gunboat the Portuguese immediately capitulated, recognising British claims to the lake. It was a minor action but one that was vital to the survival and expansion of the British Empire.

Other Pembroke Dock ships achieved fame through exploration and voyages of discovery. The cutter *Starling* had been launched as early in Pembroke Dock's history as October 1829 but she was the vessel that was used to survey the waters around Hong Kong. Her name lives on in Starling Inlet. The *Zealous* of 1864 was the first armoured ship ever to cross the Equator. Two years after her launch she became the first armoured vessel to enter the Pacific.

The ice-cold waters of the Antarctic and Arctic also saw the keels of several Pembroke Dock ships. The *Erebus*, launched in 1826 as a bomb ship, was converted to take part in Sir John Franklin's expedition to find the North-West Passage. Commanded by Sir James Clark Ross, the *Erebus* had already ventured into the southern Polar regions, the 12,400 foot volcano Mount Erebus being named after the little ship. Four years later she sailed with Franklin and was lost on the ill-fated mission. The *Alert* (1856) went to the Arctic in 1875, wintering at Floeberg Beach, the highest point of latitude then reached by man.

Some of the ships built in the dockyard had undeniably poor reputations. In some cases it was not just poor design. The *Edinburgh*, launched on 18 May 1882, was unusual in that she had a very shallow draught to enable

Before the days of photography, newspapers like *The Illustrated London News* regularly sent artists to record the launches at Royal Dockyards like Pembroke Dock. This drawing from the paper shows the Chief Constructor explaining the design of the battleship *Edinburgh* to the visiting Duchess of Edinburgh. A hotel in the town was renamed The Royal Edinburgh to commemorate the occasion of the launch and the visit of the Royal couple.

THE ILLUSTRATED LONDON NEWS

REGISTERED AT THE GENERAL POST-OFFICE FOR TRANSMISSION ABROAD.

No. 2238.—VOL. LXXX.   SATURDAY, MARCH 25, 1882.   WITH SUPPLEMENT AND COLOURED PICTURE | SIXPENCE. By Post, 6½D.

The front page of *The Illustrated London News* showing the dockyard in March 1882.

her to sail through the Suez Canal. Never totally satisfactory, by 1906, when she had been in service for over twenty years, *Jane's Fighting Ships* was describing her as:

> A poor steamer and of very little, if any, value, she is used now only for harbour service.

Another Pembroke Dock vessel, the *Thunderer*, was significant in that she was the first mastless turret ship. Her design at first evoked considerable criticism from traditionalist sailors but this was soon dispelled by her excellent sailing qualities and by the fact that she was a good gun platform. Admiral Colcomb remarked that she was:

> That steady old rock which nothing disturbs.

However, the *Thunderer* was always something of a rogue. A boiler explosion while she was on trials in Stokes Bay in 1876 killed 45 sailors. As if

that was not enough, the double charging of one of her muzzle-loading guns while on exercise in the Sea of Marmara in 1879 led to another serious accident. The barrel burst and this time 11 of the turret crew were killed.

The *Iron Duke*, a central battery ironclad of 14 guns, had been launched on St David's Day, 1870. She had the misfortune to ram and sink her sister ship *Vanguard* in a fog off the coast of Ireland in 1875. Luckily, however, the only fatality was that of a pet dog on the ill-fated *Vanguard*.

Some disasters occurred rather closer to home. When the 50-gun *Immortalite* was launched on 25 October 1859 a violent storm was already brewing out in the west. That evening it hit the town of Pembroke Dock with incredible fury and power. Three townspeople lost their lives during the night and it was considered by the dockyard workers, always a super-stitious breed of men, to be an unlucky omen for the ship. As it turned out their worries and fears were without foundation. The *Immortalite* swung easily against her jetty, safe and secure. She went on to perform admirable service for her Queen and country.

The storm that hit Pembroke Dock that night was one of the worst to ever hurl itself against the Welsh coast, the steamer *Royal Charter* being wrecked on the north Wales coast during the gale. Over 450 passengers

A wonderful panoramic view of the dockyard, taken from the Hut Encampment at Llanion. It shows a visiting torpedo boat squadron and its escorting light cruiser moored in the waterway. The Admiralty tug *Alligator* lies alongside Hobbs Point while a cruiser, probably the *Warrior*, is being fitted out at the nearby Carr Jetty.

and crew lost their lives in the disaster and the storm is still known as 'The Royal Charter Gale'. No less a personage than Charles Dickens visited north Wales to write an account of the shipwreck.

The cruiser *Thames* went down the slipway on 3 December 1885. While her engines were being tested alongside the Hobbs Point fitting-out berth, a small yacht, the *May*, full of eager spectators on their way down the Haven to see the visiting Channel Fleet, came too close and was dragged towards the cruiser by the enormous suction from the cruiser's propellers. Before anyone realised quite what was happening, the *May* was down by the stern and taking on water. Within a few minutes the tiny yacht had been struck by the giant propellers and sunk beneath the waves.

On board the yacht at the time were the owner, William Ribbon, Edwin Traylor, a local sailor by the name of Captain Greenland and several other well-known dignitaries. As the *May* went down Greenland grabbed Edwin Traylor and threw him overboard, then leapt into the water himself. William Ribbon was rescued, with difficulty, but young William Bray, another passenger on the yacht, was drowned, despite Greenland's efforts to save him. His body was not recovered for several days. Captain Greenland was later presented with a gold watch and a medal in the town's Temperance Hall as a token and reward for his bravery.

Interestingly, the *Thames* – built as a protected cruiser with two 8 inch and ten 6 inch guns – was later converted into one of the navy's first submarine depot ships. She returned to Milford Haven in 1904, taking part in general exercises in the Dale Roads and Bay area with early submarines of the Holland Class.

The *Hazard* was the yard's first torpedo gunboat to be launched with her machinery on board in February 1894. While serving on board the ship, Staff-Surgeon Maillard of Pembroke won a Victoria Cross during action around the island of Crete. He was the first naval surgeon to be awarded the VC. The *Hazard* was another vessel that came back to the Haven, escorting the Navy's first submarines into the waterway at the end of the nineteenth century.

Mrs Peters, in her seminal history of the town, quotes the improbable instance of a weird and wonderful mirage which, seemingly, occurred on the launch of the two gunboats *Gadfly* and *Pincher* on 5 May 1879:

> When these gunboats were floated the inverted image of one of them, by the rare occurrence in our country of a mirage, appeared above the steeple of St Mary's Church, Tenby, at twelve miles distance ... whether the mirage appeared to the naked eye or was only brought

out by the development of the photograph is not quite certain as statements with regard to such are somewhat contradictory.

Even in deepest, darkest west Wales, it seems, early photographic fakers were at work!

The supernatural and all that it suggested were dear to the hearts of most Victorians, no matter how rational and clear thinking they might otherwise have been. One story, intimately connected with Pembroke Dock, usually called 'The Ghost and HMS Asp', sums up the attitude of people at the time to things they neither felt totally comfortable with, nor really understood. And yet, when you read the tale, there does seem to be a degree of perverse enjoyment in the piece, both from the teller and for the readers – even then, it seems, people enjoyed having the hair on the back of their necks stand up in fright.

The survey vessel HMS *Asp* was not built at Pembroke Dockyard but she was one of many ships repaired or refitted in the yards over the years. On 15 September 1869 her commander, Captain Aldridge, wrote a letter to *The Pembroke County Guardian*, telling the story of the ghost on board his ship. Captain Aldridge took over the *Asp* at Pembroke Dock where she was about to undergo repairs:

> On taking possession of her, the Captain Superintendent remarked to me, 'Do you know, sir, your ship is said to be haunted, and I don't know if you will get any of the Dockyard men to work on her.' I, of course, smiled, and said 'I don't care for ghosts and I dare say I shall get her all to rights fast enough.'

In due course the *Asp* sailed for the River Dee and the celebrated hauntings began. Noises from the stern cabin, drawers being opened and closed, the sound of a percussion cap being snapped close to the Captain's head as he lay in his bunk – they were just the beginning:

> One night, when the vessel was at anchor ... I was woken by the quartermaster begging me to come on deck as the look-out man had rushed to the lower deck, saying that a figure of a lady was standing on the paddle box pointing with her finger to Heaven.

The Captain, being a practical man, ordered the quartermaster to send the look-out back on deck. However, when the man was given the order he immediately went into violent convulsions and the Captain himself was forced to carry out the remainder of the watch.

After that the apparition was often seen, always with her finger pointed towards the sky. Several crewmen ran screaming from the ship in fear, others refused to serve again on board the *Asp* and the Captain had no option but to let them go. Matters came to a head when the ship was brought, once again, to Pembroke Dock for repairs in 1857. The vessel was moored to the dockyard wall that first evening and all seemed well until a sentry on the dockside suddenly saw a lady mount the paddle box of the *Asp*, her hand pointed clearly up towards the heavens. In his letter to *The Pembroke County Guardian*, Captain Aldridge continued his tale about the vision and the sentry:

> She then stepped ashore and came along the path towards him when he brought his musket to the charge. 'Who goes there?' But the figure walked through the musket, upon which he dropped it and ran for the guardhouse.

Other soldiers also saw the apparition, one of them firing his musket to raise the alarm. The figure glided on until it reached the ruins of the old Paterchurch tower. There it stood with its finger to Heaven until, suddenly, she vanished from sight. That was the last sighting of the ghost on board HMS *Asp* but thanks to Captain Aldridge's letter (reprinted in the newspaper thirty years later) the story has gone down in Pembroke Dock folklore.

There was never any explanation of the vision but Captain Aldridge did offer the suggestion that, some years before, the *Asp* had been used as a mail packet between Port Patrick and Donaghadee. The body of a young woman, he claimed, had been discovered in the aft cabin, throat cut and lying on the bunk. Nobody was ever convicted of the crime. It all makes compelling reading!

Disaster was never far away from sailors in these times. The death rate among sailors, Royal and Merchant Navy alike, was frighteningly high and, in 1861 alone, Board of Trade figures show that it stood at one in 56 of all those who went to sea. Falling from masts, being lost overboard and, of course, the risk from fire were all significant hazards. Apart from the *Clarence* and *Royal William* on the Mersey, the *Imogene*, launched at Pembroke Dock in 1831 and a respected veteran of the Chinese opium wars, was destroyed by fire at Devonport Dockyard in September 1840.

Perhaps most tragic of all was the loss of the training ship *Atalanta* in February 1880. The use of wooden training ships where boys could learn to coil ropes, steer ships and climb masts was common during the Victorian age. Many of these training vessels were old wooden battleships,

H.M.S. AMPHION.

stationary vessels moored in estuaries around the country. Some, however, were sea-going vessels and the *Atalanta*, launched under the name *Juno* from Pembroke Dockyard in 1844, was one of these. She left Bermuda on 1 February and foundered with all hands in the North Atlantic some days later. Her crew of 113 and 170 young trainees went down with the ship. A stained-glass window was set into the Dockyard Chapel to commemorate the loss.

No fewer than five of the Cherokee class sloops built at the dockyard in the 1820s and 1830s were lost at sea. Some, like the *Skylark* and *Spey*, were wrecked on the Isle of Wight and Racoon Key in the Bahamas respectively. Others simply disappeared without trace. The *Thais*, for example, was lost while on passage to Halifax in 1833, while the *Camilla* went down off the coast of Japan nearly thirty years later.

When the world erupted into mayhem in August 1914, Pembroke Dock ships were immediately involved. The light cruiser *Amphion* was the first British ship to be sunk during the war, mined in the North Sea on 6 August 1914. Two years later U52 torpedoed the *Nottingham*, again in the North Sea. The *Drake*, the longest ship ever to be launched from the yards, was also torpedoed at about the same time. In the final year of the war the torpedo gunboat *Hazard* was also sunk when she was involved in a collision off Portland.

The cruiser *Amphion* was launched on 4 December 1911. She was the first British warship to be lost in the Great War.

It was the Battle of Jutland, however, that brought the greatest blow to the ships of Pembroke Dock. *Warrior* (1905) *Defence* (1907) and the *Duke of Edinburgh* (1904), together with the *Black Prince*, made up the 1st Cruiser Squadron under the command of Rear Admiral Sir Robert Arbuthnot who flew his flag in the *Defence*. Shortly after 18.00 hours, in the early stages of the battle, the 1st Cruiser Squadron was pursuing a German scout group when, out of the haze, loomed Admiral Hipper's battlecruisers and the seven dreadnoughts of the German 3rd Battle Squadron. Before the British ships could turn away, the Germans immediately opened fire on the startled cruisers.

Defence was hit by a German salvo at precisely 18.15 hours and a huge red flame flashed up from abaft her rear turret. The ship seemed to stagger and heel over but quickly righted herself and ploughed onwards. Almost immediately, she was hit by another salvo, between the foremost turret and first funnel, and was lost to sight in an enormous cloud of black smoke. When the smoke had cleared the ship had disappeared. Admiral Arbuthnot and almost 900 men had gone with her.

In this classic photograph the cruiser *Defence* has just entered the water on 27 April 1907. Look at the workman in the foreground – he turns away to get on with the job. He has undoubtedly seen it all before.

Now fitted out with guns, engines and funnels, *Defence* is brought alongside the berth.

HMS *Defence* with an Admiralty tug alongside, just after her launch. *Defence* was one of several Pembroke Dock ships sunk at the Battle of Jutland.

The *Warrior* was hit by 15 heavy shells from the German battlecruisers and lost steam from her engines. Within minutes she was on fire, her upper deck a shambles, and listing sharply to starboard. Only the timely intervention of the battleship *Warspite* saved her and by 19.00 hours she had been taken in tow by a seaplane carrier. Trying to save the stricken *Warrior* was a fruitless exercise, particularly as during the night the weather

HMS *Duke of Edinburgh* was an armoured cruiser launched in January 1904.

worsened and her stern sank lower and lower into the water. The seaplane carrier came alongside and took off the surviving crew. Shortly afterwards the *Warrior* sank.

In the unequal contest with the German battlecruisers the *Black Prince* was also sunk. Only the *Duke of Edinburgh* from the 1st Cruiser Squadron escaped destruction. In addition to the two Pembroke Dock ships, numerous sailors from the town lost their lives, either on the *Defence*, *Warrior* or *Black Prince*.

The dockyard built a number of small submarines during the war years. Of these, the L10 was sunk by a German destroyer off Texal in the final months of the war. She had led an eventful, if short, life. Launched in January 1918, in March she was engaged in diving trials off St Anne's Head and failed to surface after touching the bottom. Several dockyard men were on board for the trials, including Arthur Ball, Charge Hand Shipwright, and Frederick Vivian Hay and John Thomas of Llangwm. The last two were the fathers of Viv Hay, the renowned Quins player and committee man, and Llewellyn Thomas, a noted local journalist. Luckily for everyone, the fault on board L10 was eventually located and, after several hours, the submarine rose to the surface once more. Off Texal, on active service later in the year, she was not so fortunate.

The light cruiser *Curacoa*, built in 1918, survived the Great War only to perish during the Second World War when she was involved in a collision

HMS *Curacoa*, launched from the yards in May 1917, was sunk during the Second World War when she was hit by the liner *Queen Mary* and cut in two.

with the giant Cunard liner *Queen Mary* off the coast of Ireland. At the time the *Curacoa* was engaged on convoy escort duties and the *Queen Mary*, normally used to making fast, unescorted trips across the Atlantic, cut the cruiser in half. All but twenty-six of the *Curacoa's* crew were lost in the accident.

An interesting story about the *Victoria and Albert* of 1899 concerns her eventual demise. In keeping with tradition during her construction two golden sovereigns had been placed beneath one of her masts, the coins having been donated by the Pembroke Borough Council. When the yacht was finally broken up in 1955 the Town Clerk was instructed to write to the Queen, asking for the sovereigns to be returned. The palace, not unnaturally, refused the request but sent the Council a teak cigarette box made from the timber of the old *V & A*. The box is still kept in Pembroke Town Hall.

Pembroke Dock ships were built for a purpose, either to wage war or to supply those ships that were involved in combat. There is no doubt that they performed their tasks admirably. They brought glory and fame to both the town and the dockyard and it is fitting that they should, therefore, be remembered.

CHAPTER SEVEN

The Town Grows

FROM ITS INCEPTION IN 1814 Pembroke Dock was the only truly industrial town in the whole of Pembrokeshire. It was created to build ships and, unlike its neighbours Pembroke and Haverfordwest, had little inclination to being thought of as a market town or agricultural centre. Smaller communities such as Neyland, just across the river from the dockyard, might have had pretensions to industrial status but, really, the place never came close. Even Milford, with its fishing industry, could not compete with its big brother just up river.

An aerial view of the town.

PEMBROKE DOCK *from the Air*

By 1848 the town of Pembroke Dock was flourishing around the dockyard walls, a certain impetus to the yards having been given by the continental revolutions that year. In the early years the town had been unlighted and anyone venturing out of doors after dark would have to find his way by using a hand lantern. A man by the name of John Richards introduced gas to the town, around about the year 1853, the original gas works being situated to the south of the dockyard walls. Richards was, for some time, the sole owner of the town's gas works until he sold it to the County and General Gas Company of London. The premises of Mr William Laen, a chemist in Meyrick Street, were the first to be lit by gas, many of the town's inhabitants happily standing on the pavement outside the shop to admire the spectacle.

Collections or subscription lists were circulated for the purpose of providing gas lamps for the streets before the Council declared that Commercial Row and Pembroke Street should be lit by gas lamps. The gas rate for the first year was, apparently, only three pence in the pound. The following year, however, the figure was doubled. Gas was bought from Mr Richards and, after he sold the operation, from the new company. At the end of the nineteenth century the gas works was owned by the Pembroke Dock and Towns Gas Company, shares being offered for public sale in 1903 and 1904.

The population of the town increased steadily throughout the nineteenth century. The census returns for 1841 gave the total population for St Mary's parish – and it must be remembered that that included part of nearby Pembroke – as 5,441. By 1871 that figure had risen to a staggering 12,000 as artisans and tradesmen flocked to the area to work in the dockyard. By 1901 the population figure stood at 13,000 while in the early 1920s it had risen to 15,460.

In order to meet the needs of this growing population a whole range of services had to provided, both formally and unofficially. To begin with there were public houses. The dramatic and wonderfully evocative picture has often been drawn of 30 or 40 pints of beer sitting in a row, waiting for dockyard workers at the end of their shift, on the bars of places like the Navy Inn or the Charlton. And that image is, in the main, quite true. It was difficult, thirsty work in the dockyard, particularly in places like the saw pits or the foundries, and the men needed to both slake their thirst and unwind after a hard day's work.

Sometimes, however, things became more than a little unsavoury, particularly when you added soldiers to the mix. There are many recorded

Bufferland, one of several small communities clustered around the town, has always regarded itself as a separate entity from the main part of Pembroke Dock.

BUFFERLAND.

instances of fights and riots in the town when respectable citizens undoubtedly raised their eyes to heaven and literally ran for their lives.

The Landshipping Inn was located in Queen Street, operating as both a pub and lodging house. In 1868 it was the scene of an attempted murder when James Thomas stabbed soldier James Gafney in the back yard of the pub. There must have been extenuating circumstances in the affair, however, as Thomas was acquitted of the assault at the next quarter sessions. The landlords and landladies themselves were no shrinking violets, either. In 1862 Thomas Owen and his daughter Margaret Evans of the Milford Arms in Commercial Row were taken to court, accused of having administered a sound thrashing to a sailor from HMS *Lucifer* – an appropriate name, perhaps – who had tried to leave the pub without settling his bar bill.

In 1876 the Old Lion in King Street, one of the oldest public houses in the town, was the scene of a full scale riot when soldiers of the 54th Dorsetshire Regiment celebrated their last night in the town before being posted to Ireland. The soldiers engaged in what, these days, would be called 'a pub crawl' before finally congregating, late at night, in King Street. Some of them then smashed their way into the Old Lion where they promptly proceeded to wreck the place. Glasses were smashed and chairs thrown through windows in a scene more reminiscent of a Hollywood western than a town in west Wales. When the police eventually regained order 40 soldiers spent the rest of the night either in jail or in the military cells of the Defensible Barracks and the Hut Encampment at Llanion.

Another riot occurred in the Castle Inn, a public house then located in Clarence Street, in the summer of 1861. Fifty soldiers charged into the pub and, seemingly without any real cause or reason, began to smash up the place. They caused over £50 worth of damage but, surprisingly, the pub stayed open for business.

There had been Sunday closing for pubs in Wales since the Welsh Sunday Closing Act of 1881. However, the law was often flouted, as Keith Johnson records in his book *The Pubs of Pembroke, Pembroke Dock, Tenby and South Pembrokeshire* with regard to the King's Arms in Front Street:

> One day, during the summer of that year [1889], two policemen lurking in the Gun Tower kept the house under observation, from 8 am until dusk and counted over 80 customers visiting the pub. This would have been fine, except for the fact that it was a Sunday and the pub was meant to be closed.

The publican, William Horn, duly lost his licence at the next Brewster Sessions!

Another Front Street pub was the scene of a horrific accident and death in 1861. Mrs Ruth Davies from the Sailors Return was burned to death when she reached up to place something on the mantelpiece and her crinoline brushed against the coals of the lighted fire. Before anyone could move she was a mass of flames. Mrs Davies later died from her injuries. While the story is horrifying to modern readers, such deaths were probably more common in Victorian Britain than people realise but the incident does appear to have been the first known death by fire in Pembroke Dock.

Cottages at Llanion. Pedestrians could climb over the stile, cross the railway line and walk along Bird Cage Walk into town.

With the advent of soldiers – single men or, at least, married men stationed well away from their wives – came the inevitable 'ladies of the night', prostitutes who peddled their wares in back alleys and in the less salubrious of the town's public houses. There are many recorded instances of prostitution in Pembroke Dock, local papers of the time being full of the fight to curb the problem. It remains a far from edifying part of the town's history but was inevitable when you consider the make-up of so much of the male population in the years when the town was thriving and growing at a rate that would have amazed the founders of the dockyard back in 1814.

The Rising Sun public house stood at the bottom of Brewery Street and was renowned as a 'waiting room' where soldiers would queue for their turn in a nearby brothel. The brothel, incidentally, was closed after a police raid in 1913. The Devonport Inn, close by in Queen Street, was also known as a place to pick up prostitutes, as was the Castle in nearby Clarence Street. In 1878 the landlord of the Devonport, John Price, was fined £2 for allowing his premises to become the 'haunt of known prostitutes'. As late as 1912, Harold Kennedy, the landlord of the Navy Tavern in Pembroke Street, was similarly hauled before the magistrates, charged with allowing his pub to be used as a brothel.

Keith Johnson quotes an interesting exchange that sums up the attitudes of authority to the problem of prostitution in these years. William Williams, a shoemaker in the town, made a complaint that he had been robbed of just over eleven shillings by a prostitute in the Crystal Palace pub in Market Street:

> the magistrates dismissed the case. 'If you frequent such houses you deserve to be robbed,' they admonished him. Williams was forced to pay 1s. 6d. costs – which he did 'amidst much tittering in the court.'

The Royal Marines in Upper Park Street was, as its name suggests, well frequented by the soldiers of Pembroke Dock. In the 1860s and 1870s it was also renowned as the regular drinking place for two infamous town prostitutes called Queenstown Ellen and Sally Duff, exotic and fascinating names that hide the base nature of what was on offer from the two women. At this distance it is hard to make judgements about Victorian prostitution. Were the women victims of society? Or did they prey on the lusts of lonely men, many miles from home and family? There is no easy answer.

Of course, not all Pembroke Dock hostelries were places of corruption and rowdiness. Some were exceptionally clean and well-run, a pleasure to enter. They were places where anyone could enjoy a few hours of idleness and good companionship. The twin houses of the Clarence Inn and Victoria Hotel were classic examples of good, well-run taverns. The Victoria even possessed a ballroom. In 1882 the Royal Hotel in Queen Street was renamed the Royal Edinburgh after the Duke and Duchess of Edinburgh launched a battleship of that name from the dockyard. The Royal Edinburgh boasted stables and coach houses, smoking rooms, coffee rooms and a number of large function rooms. Situated in the centre of town it was, for a long time, the premier hotel in Pembroke Dock and traded for well over a hundred years.

Rowdiness and prostitution were not the only problems facing the town. There was also the major issue of public health. An adequate supply of good, fresh water for the people of the town was, for many years, a major priority.

Many of the early houses had open tanks attached to them, the purpose being to catch and collect rain water for both drinking and washing. One or two of the houses even had private wells in their gardens but the tenants or owners of these properties were undoubtedly the lucky ones. For many years the only source of fresh water came from various wells of spring water around the town. One of these was called Fountain Well, located at the top of South Park Street – for many years it was uncovered and therefore open to all manner of pollution. Other wells around the town included Fortland Well at Llanion, Rock Well, close to Hobbs Point, and Cambrian Well which lay on the eastern side of Tregenna's Hill.

Some of the streets nearest to the dockyard were lucky as they were supplied with water from the Government Reservoirs located at the foot of Tregenna's Hill. The reservoirs had been built with earth taken from the top of the hill when the Defensible Barracks had been built and while undoubtedly efficient were really intended solely for use within the dockyard.

Towards the end of the nineteenth century various projects were carried out in an attempt to improve the water supply. These included the boring of a tunnel into the ridge above the town, close to Prospect Place, in order to tap into the various springs that had their sources there. The water was then collected in reservoirs. Hydrants were placed on a number of streets in the town, water being conveyed to them through pipes from the reservoirs. Eventually, as the nineteenth century drew to a close, a new waterworks was built at Milton, some seven or eight miles to the east of

Owen Street in Pennar, one of several streets in the little suburb that was badly hit by a cholera outbreak in 1865 and 1866.

the town, and water was at last brought through pipes to the houses of the town and to the dockyard.

These days the need for good public health and adequate sanitation is clear to everyone. In the early days of Pembroke Dock this was not the case. On three separate occasions there were outbreaks of smallpox in the town, the first epidemic being centred on Queen Street in the 1850s. The source of the outbreak was thought to have been a batch of second-hand clothing that had been bought in Swansea and subsequently brought to the town.

The outlying community of Pennar was badly affected by severe cholera outbreaks in the years 1865 and 1866, the lack of a clean water supply being the cause of the outbreak. Mrs Peters might have been stretching the truth a little when she commented on the outbreaks in her book *The History of Pembroke Dock,* but her words do catch the mood of the moment:

> So malignant was the complaint that mourners not infrequently returned from the funeral of one relative to find another of the family had been stricken by the dread disease.

As if cholera was not enough, Pennar was promptly hit by an outbreak of scarlet fever in 1867, the year after the second cholera epidemic. Smallpox visited the place in 1892 and, in 1919 in the wake of the Great War, it was

The *Saturn*, one time Guardship at Pembroke Dock.

Before the town's hospital was built, an old wooden-wall, the *Nankin,* served as an infirmary and hospital. This 1880 view of the Haven shows her and the Admiralty tug *Stormcock.*

ravaged by the outbreak of influenza that spread like wildfire across the whole of Europe. A diphtheria epidemic followed in the 1920s.

For many years there was no hospital in the town of Pembroke Dock. To begin with an old wooden warship, the *Saturn,* was used to care for sick or injured dockyard workers. The Admiralty was clear, only dockyard workers were eligible for admission. She was replaced by the *Nankin* in 1866, dealing chiefly with the industrial injuries that were common in the dockyard. A picturesque sight from the shore, conditions on board the old wooden-wall were not quite so pleasant. She was eventually taken from her moorings off the dockyard on 18 April 1895 and towed to Milford where she was duly broken up. A small hospital was then created to care for injured men within the dockyard walls.

The foundation stone of the Meyrick Wards and Nurses' Home was laid in North Park Street on 12 April 1898 to commemorate Queen Victoria's Diamond Jubilee. S.J. Allen, photographer of the town and dockyard, the man to whom we owe so many great visual records, was Mayor at the time and much of the credit for the new hospital has to go to him. However, the building was far too small for a town the size of Pembroke Dock, only sixteen beds being provided. Nevertheless, it continued to operate for many years, offering a specific service as a maternity hospital and only finally closing its doors in 1961. Even then the old building continued to be of use, operating as a clinic and a base for social workers until it was demolished and the site redeveloped in the 1990s.

The old mould loft of Jacobs Pill Dockyard, a private yard close to Bufferland and Pennar, was converted into an isolation hospital for the town after the small yard closed in the late 1880s. By 1923 this building had 14 beds and was taken over by the County Council in 1925. By the 1940s it was too old and obsolete to be of any real use and was closed down.

The Victoria Nurses' Home and Meyrick Wards, in Park Street, were built between 1898 and 1899 and were paid for by public subscription. This S.J. Allen postcard shows the crowd at the opening of the new operating theatre at the hospital in 1911.

OPENING OPERATING THEATRE.
1911

Once the Meyrick Hos[...] [...] Riverside Hospital in Pembroke
became the main maternit[...] unit in the area, countless Pembroke Dock
mothers giving birth to [...] [...] [...] wards. Interestingly, the
Riverside site had original[...] b[...] the property of the Pembroke
Dock never had its own Poor Law Institution and, being part of the
Borough of Pembroke, an[...] [...] poor [...] they were forced
to seek shelter and solace in the near[...] town of Pembroke.

A new Admiralty hos[...] on Fort [...] outside the dockyard gates,
was completed in 1902. Covering an area of [...] or six acres, the
building cost approxima[...] [...] [...] considered to be the most
advanced hospital facilit[...] in the county. The new hospital was only for
Admiralty employees, however, and even after the dockyard closed in
1926 it remained under Admiralty control. Some of the wards were used
as isolation units during the various scarlet fever and diphtheria outbreaks
but even during the Second World War the place was still reserved for
Royal Navy personnel. Only in the years after the war did it become a
public facility.

Before Forster's Education Act of 1870 there was no compulsory
education in Britain. That did not mean there were no schools, but those
that were in existence were of a voluntary nature. Provision and standards
were, at best, patchy and the system – or, really, lack of system – meant that
the rich were well catered for in their great public schools; the criminal
classes were looked after in the reformatories and industrial schools; but
for the honest and ordinary boy and girl in the street there was next to
nothing on offer.

Pembroke Dock's first schoolmaster was a certain John Allen, a man
who had previously farmed land at Lawrenny. Realising that farming
presented few opportunities, Allen changed his career and, assisted by his
son John and daughter Elizabeth, opened a small school in King Street in
the early years of the town's history. Apparently, many of the boys taught
at Allen's school later went to work in the new dockyard and did very
well indeed.

According to Mrs Peters there were several small voluntary schools
in the town during these early years. They included one kept by a Mr
Isaacs in Charlton Place and Mr Tregenna'a establishment in a large room,
built for the purpose, in a building opposite Bethany Chapel at the top
of Tregenna's Hill. Other schools were run by people like Mrs Bennett,
Tom Morris, Mrs Raynes and Mr Newman. The latter was remembered
in the town for many years, a real character and someone who enthralled

This shows Victoria Road and one of the town's first important schools, the National School which opened its doors for the first time in 1845.

local boys because of his wooden leg. He had lost his own leg during an engagement between his ship, the frigate *Shannon,* and the American *Chesapeake* many years before.

Despite increasing disquiet in the press and in Parliament over evils like infant labour and widespread illiteracy, during the 1820s and 1830s the government steadfastly refused to become involved with the provision of education. Such provision was, largely, left to charities and voluntary agencies. There was a significant gap in provision, and it was into this gap that two of the most influential religious agencies of the nineteenth century now stepped. They were the British and Foreign School Society, founded on the inspiration of Quaker Joseph Lancaster, and the National Society for Promoting Education of the Poor in the Principles of the Established Church.

The first major school in the town was created in 1845 when Francis Allen and his wife Maria flung open the doors of the National School in Victoria Road. A large fête had been held in the dockyard when the 80-gun *Superb* was launched in September 1842, its sole purpose being to raise money for the creation of this new school. Although the school was voluntary, the government still wanting no say in the provision or running of education, the Admiralty and officers from the dockyard had been fully involved in the foundation of the school. Captain Jackson, the Captain Superintendent of the yards, and Master Shipwright William Edye were both members of the committee formed to establish the school and the government even went so far as to donate the land on which the buildings soon stood.

The success of the National School was immediate and lasting. When William Morris, a Schools Inspector, visited the place in 1847 – as part of the wide-ranging series of inspections that strongly criticised the state of education in Wales, the Treason of the Blue Books, as the report is now universally known – the National School at Pembroke Dock received considerable praise. The lure of good jobs in the nearby dockyard, Morris felt, was a major impetus for hard work. Other Pembroke Dock schools were not so fortunate.

Miss Slocomb's school in Park Street was given particularly short shrift. The schoolmistress was discovered plastering up a wall while her charges gazed on or amused themselves in the best way they could. The children were cold and uncared for and Miss Slocomb herself was mostly ignorant of the basic principles of education. Small wonder, then, that the Blue Books condemned the state of education in the Principality.

The National School's success quickly brought overcrowding. As late as 1906, long after compulsory education had been introduced, the school still had a roll of nearly 400 students. In the years just after its foundation, however, it was feared that Church of England doctrines were being taught to many of the nonconformist children who attended the school, mainly because there was nowhere else for them to go if they wanted a good

my 2nd) Gramor School.

County School, Pembroke Dock.

The County Intermediate School was established in the town under the provision of the Welsh Intermediate Education Act of 1889. In its later days the building became the town Grammar School and, eventually, the upper school of the Coronation Secondary Modern.

standard of education. Therefore, a concert was held on 1 May 1846 with the aim of raising funds to create a British School in the town.

Despite part of the roof collapsing during the construction, the new British School was duly opened in Meyrick Street in 1848. Under the guidance of Mr and Mrs Adams the school made excellent progress and when Matthew Arnold, operating as one of Her Majesty's Inspectors, visited the establishment he declared it to be the best school in Wales for the teaching of Mathematics.

The old British School was pulled down in the early years of the twentieth century and the famous Coronation School opened in its place on 4 May 1904. On opening day children from all the schools in town, clad in their best clothes and distinctive coloured ribbons, marched from Albion Square to the new school where they were all presented with tins of chocolates, the lids of which bore a portrait of the King. It was felt to be important to garner a degree of enthusiasm for education amongst the town's children. For several years the Log Books of schools like the National had been complaining about the number of absentees, particularly when a ship was launched from the dockyard or, even more significantly, during the potato-picking season on the nearby farms.

The County Intermediate School was established in the town under the provision of the Welsh Intermediate Education Act of 1889. Built on the corner of Bush Street and Argyle Street between 1897 and 1899, it was run under the auspices of the Central Welsh Board of Education and in 1904 was extended to include a large physics lab and central hall. In later years the premises became the town's grammar school and, late in its history, the senior section of the Coronation Secondary Modern.

A year after Forster's Education Act in 1870 the Pembroke School Board was formed. By 1873 they had taken over the British School and, because of the size of Pembroke Dock, were already planning more elementary schools in the town. Pennar School opened on 5 January 1874 while Albion Square began its work three years later. In 1892 another school was opened in Llanion.

The Dockyard Class had always been important in Pembroke Dock. In the early days of the yards apprentices were taught on board the old *Dragon* but the creation of a Dockyard Class for those boys who wanted to apply for an apprenticeship in the yards was a natural progression. For a while this class was held in the National School but after Albion Square school was opened in 1877 it quickly became the site for the class. By the closing years of the century the Dockyard Class had become the highest echelon in an establishment that the Pembroke Dock School Board ensured was equipped to the best possible standard. From 1887 onwards Albion Square School was offering subjects such as chemistry, mechanics and magnetism.

In addition to their work during the school day, students for the Civil Service Examination for Dockyard Apprentices were required to attend classes every evening from 6.00 until 7.45 p.m. Competition for places in the yards was exceptionally high. Each of the Royal Naval Dockyards – Chatham, Portsmouth, Pembroke Dock, Devonport, and Haulbowline in Ireland – had their own quotas for apprentices needed in the various trades and vacancies, naturally, varied each year. Only the top students could be sure of gaining an apprenticeship. Admission to the Dockyard Class was not something to be taken lightly and, indeed, was an honour coveted by most of the boys from Pembroke Dock.

In the years after 1850 new streets were developed to cater for the growing population. These included roads like Arthur Street (supposedly named after an agent of Sir Thomas Meyrick), Apley Terrace and Argyle Street. On 22 April 1872 an Order was made that, as of that summer, the County Court should be held at Pembroke Dock rather than Pembroke. The town was growing in both size and significance and, to its residents and to visitors alike, the future looked decidedly prosperous.

CHAPTER EIGHT

Captains and Kings

Workmen on board
a visiting ship in the
early 1900s.

A s w e h a v e s e e n, following the amalgamation of the Navy
and Admiralty Boards in 1832, naval officers were for the first
time appointed to take charge of all Royal Naval Dockyards. All of the
major dockyards were to be governed by Admiral Superintendents and
it is perhaps significant – an indication of the way that the Lords of the
Admiralty felt about their Welsh yard – that Pembroke Dock should
warrant only a Captain Superintendent.

Within the dockyards the Admiral or Captain Superintendent's word was law. He was, literally, lord of all he surveyed. He lived in the dockyard, surrounded by his officers, and was always on hand should things require his immediate attention. His was real power, to wield and use as and when he wanted. Most of the Admirals and Captain Superintendents, however, had little or no knowledge about the actual art of shipbuilding. In some instances this led to a degree of friction. As Lawrence Phillips has commented:

> These sea officers had no shipbuilding knowledge and there was often tension between them and their civilian Master Shipwrights, later Chief Constructors, who had spent a lifetime in the trade. These senior captains, however, knew about handling men.

That certainly applied to some of the Captain Superintendents at Pembroke Dock, but perhaps not to all of them. Pembroke Dockyard had thirty-five Superintendents between the amalgamation in 1832 and closure in 1926. They were officially attached to the various guard ships positioned out in the Haven, vessels such as the *Bellerophon*, *Rupert*, *Thunderer* and *Hood*, and were obviously something of a mixed bag. Some of them were loved and admired by their men, others were certainly not.

Clearly fitting into this last category was Sir Watkin Owen Pell who was Captain Superintendent between 1842 and 1845. He was renowned among the workforce as being something of a martinet. He had lost a leg in an engagement against the French in 1800 and, while the injury did not warrant him being pensioned off, he did find moving around quite difficult. He rectified this situation by training his pony Jack to climb and manoeuvre himself into the most awkward of positions, sometimes appearing alongside his men as they worked on the gantries and gangways. Pell is said to have regularly spied on his men through a telescope from the Barrack Hill to see if they were idling or engaging in what he considered to be illicit activities.

Perhaps such precautions were not quite as silly as they sound. The Pembroke Dock men, like those in the other Royal Dockyards, quickly developed what was known as 'the dockyard crawl', a way of dawdling along between one job and the next or whenever work was in the offing. When the dinner bell was rung – and lunch was invariably called dinner in the yards – they would change gear and quickly hurry off to their lunch boxes.

A famous dockyard rhyme, common in most of the Royal Naval yards,

The building of commemorative arches was a tradition in Victorian Britain whenever a member of the Royal family visited or, in the case of dockyard towns, when a Royal Yacht was launched.

summed up the attitude of many workers. It was a song that was often sung with self-deprecating humour by the men themselves:

> Ever seen a dockyard matie run?
> Yes, I've seen it done.
> At the sounding of the bell
> Dockyard maties run like hell.

One well-known local legend declares that there was barely a house in Pembroke Dock that did not have dockyard timber used somewhere in its construction. Dozens of greenhouses, garden sheds and pigeon coops were made entirely out of the stuff. Some of the wood was probably sneaked out, past the eyes of the Dockyard Police on the gate, but most of the men did not have to risk this rather chancy way of obtaining building materials. They would simply take the wood, suitably bound together, down to one of the slips and throw it into the water. Provided they had judged the tide correctly, the bundle would be washed up on Front Street beach where it could be easily and safely picked up after work. Whether or not this is true remains unclear but it is quite likely that the taking of reasonable quantities of wood from the yards was accepted or even condoned by most dockyard officers. Some of the more rigid disciplinarians – naval officers who had spent most of their life at sea, for example – probably found the practice a little hard to accept.

Perhaps, therefore, Pell's precautions and fears were not entirely unfounded. However, they did not make him popular with the men and when he left the yards in 1845 there was a collective sigh of relief. He went on to become Commissioner of Greenwich Hospital, a post he held until 1863. He died in 1869, some years after retirement.

Pell was not the only Captain Superintendent to doubt his workforce. Burgess Watson was in post at the end of the nineteenth century, running the yards between 1896 and 1899, the year that the *Victoria and Albert* was launched. He was another commander who was convinced that his men were idle:

> his suspicions reached a dramatic climax on 15 July 1898, when he assembled every Dockyard officer, from Chief Constructor down to the humblest chargeman in the Dockyard Schoolroom. He reported that he had found a hutch in a timber stack, roofed with corrugated iron, and equipped with towels, water and pillows and in which, it seemed, men had been going to skulk, sleep and – worse still – perhaps smoke, for weeks or months previously.

The Dockyard Police later found three men in the 'bolt hole' and they were summarily dismissed. Burgess Watson had gathered many other examples of 'shirking workmen' including one occasion when all hands ceased to work after they had heard a bell, not the official lunch hour bell but the sound of a hammer striking against iron.

The memorial plaque to William Pryce Cumby, Trafalgar veteran and one time Captain Superintendent of Pembroke Dockyard. Restored in 1974, the old town cemetery in Park Street, where the plaque holds a place of honour, is now a quiet park.

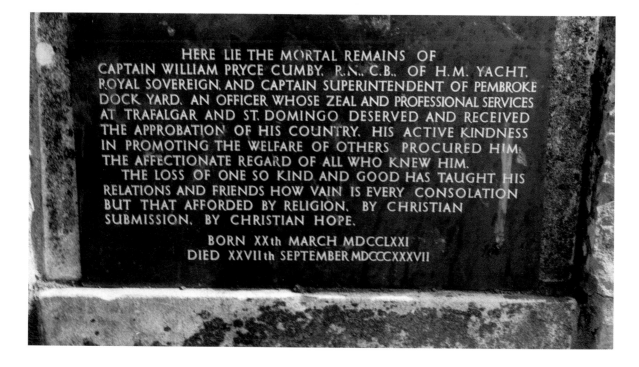

HERE LIE THE MORTAL REMAINS OF CAPTAIN WILLIAM PRYCE CUMBY, R.N., C.B., OF H.M. YACHT ROYAL SOVEREIGN, AND CAPTAIN SUPERINTENDENT OF PEMBROKE DOCK YARD. AN OFFICER WHOSE ZEAL AND PROFESSIONAL SERVICES AT TRAFALGAR AND ST. DOMINGO DESERVED AND RECEIVED THE APPROBATION OF HIS COUNTRY. HIS ACTIVE KINDNESS IN PROMOTING THE WELFARE OF OTHERS PROCURED HIM THE AFFECTIONATE REGARD OF ALL WHO KNEW HIM.
THE LOSS OF ONE SO KIND AND GOOD HAS TAUGHT HIS RELATIONS AND FRIENDS HOW VAIN IS EVERY CONSOLATION BUT THAT AFFORDED BY RELIGION, BY CHRISTIAN SUBMISSION, BY CHRISTIAN HOPE.
BORN XXth MARCH MDCCLXXI
DIED XXVIIth SEPTEMBER MDCCCXXXVII

The very first Captain Superintendent at Pembroke Dock was Sir Charles Bullen who had at one time commanded the Royal Yacht and been third-in-command of HMS *Britannia*, the naval training ship for officers at Dartmouth. He had also been Commissioner at Chatham Dockyard in Kent, so he knew at least something about the workings of Royal Naval yards. Bullen was actually knighted whilst serving at Pembroke Dock and went on to become an Admiral, dying at the great age of 86 in 1853 as the last surviving Trafalgar veteran. He was in charge at Pembroke Dock until 1837 when he was succeed by William Pryce Cumby, CB.

Like Bullen before him, Cumby was also a Trafalgar veteran. He had been First Lieutenant of the *Bellerophon*, better known in the navy by the name of *Billy Ruffian*, and had taken command when his captain, John Cooke, was killed by musket fire. Apparently the dying Cooke fell to the deck with his chest pierced by two musket balls but refused to be carried below. 'Tell Cumby never to strike!' Cooke said before he died. He need not have worried. Cumby was not the sort to haul down his colours, despite the fact that at the end of the action over a quarter of the ship's company had been killed or wounded. He actually saved many lives, and possibly the ship too, when she was engaged in mortal conflict with the French *Aigle*, by picking up a smouldering grenade and hurling it over the side. Cumby went on to command a squadron in the West Indies before coming to Pembroke Dock in 1837.

The strain of command and of withstanding the horrors of battles such as Trafalgar and St Domingo must, however, have taken their toll on Cumby. He died the same year he was appointed to the yards and was buried in the Park Street cemetery. His name lives on in the town, Cumby Terrace being named after him. A memorial plaque in the old cemetery, now rather battered and worn, records his achievements. It reads:

> Here lie the mortal remains of William Pryce Cumby, RN, CB, of HM Yacht Royal Sovereign, and Captain Superintendent of Pembroke Dockyard, an officer whose professional services at Trafalgar and St Domingo deserved and received the approbation of his country. His active kindness in promoting the welfare of others procured him the affectionate regard of all who knew him. The loss of one so kind and good has taught his relations and friends how vain is every consolation but that afforded by religion, by Christian submission, by Christian hope.

Samuel Jackson, CB, was another Nelson man. He served as Captain

THE KING AND QUEEN LANDING AT PEMBROKE DOCK.

Superintendent from 1837 until 1842, the third man to hold the position. He was already 66 years old when he was appointed and died just three years after his retirement.

Many of the Captain Superintendents inspired great loyalty from the dockyard workforce. Amongst these was Captain Sir Thomas Sabine Pasley who was cheered to the echo both by his workers and by the sailors from the guardship *Saturn* when he left the yards for the last time on board the paddle steamer *Prospero*. That was in June 1854, after he had been at the yards for almost six years. In his diary Pasley wrote:

> I shall always look back on Pembroke Yard as the most comfortable and satisfactory epoch of my life.

His memory of the farewell he had been given was also something that would be remembered:

> At last the Yard was cleared and the last sound of Pembroke Dockyard that I shall ever hear died away. But the recollection will never die from my memory. I was quite overcome and felt it all very deeply. God bless them all!

Pasley's daughter Louisa was with him during his time at Pembroke

King Edward VII visited Pembroke Dock in August 1902. This shows the King and Queen Alexandria coming ashore from the Royal Yacht at the dockyard.

Dock. She later recalled the time as an idyllic period in Paradise with no telephones to disturb either the Captain Superintendent or his staff.

Charles Penrose Fitzgerald succeeded to the Pembroke Dock post many years later, in 1893. Even as late as that, he declared the posting to be 'the very best captain's appointment in the service'. Always a harsh disciplinarian, Fitzgerald later commented that his two years as Captain Superintendent gave him a good home with an excellent garden that was, importantly, 'a long way from London and the Admiralty'.

Cumby was not the only Captain Superintendent to die in post. Captain W. H. Hall was appointed to the dockyard in 1895 but died at the Royal Edinburgh Hotel in the centre of the town that same year. Captain G. Ramsey was in command between 1857 and 1862. He subsequently became Lord Dalhousie, a name which, in an earlier generation, is perhaps better known for its connections with the Indian sub-continent. The last incumbent of the post was Leonard Donaldson whose appointment was terminated on 31 May 1926, the day that the dockyard was reduced to a Care and Maintenance Standard.

Despite the fact that Pembroke Dockyard was the navy's main building yard during her reign, Queen Victoria never visited either the town or the dockyard. She did sail into the Haven on one occasion, on board the

The huge bonfire on the Barrack Hill, built to celebrate the coronation of King George V in 1911.

first *Victoria and Albert*. That was on 14 August 1849 but the Queen did not come ashore. Many small boats set out from Pembroke Dock and other towns and villages along the Haven in order to see the royal party and Prince Albert, the Queen's consort, soon boarded the *Fairy*, a small yacht that was accompanying the *V & A*. He sailed up the Haven before landing in the dockyard.

The Prince made a quick inspection of the *Lion*, an 80-gun battleship then under construction in the yards, and drove through the town towards Bush Hill. From the top of the hill he stared for a while at nearby Pembroke Castle before returning to the *Fairy* and sailing away down the Haven.

Prince Albert returned to the area in 1859, along with his son, the future Edward VII. Then he boarded the Royal Yacht from Neyland, *en route* to Ireland, and did not come to the dockyard town. When he died two years later the town of Pembroke Dock observed a day of national mourning with the yards and all businesses firmly closed and shut up.

King Edward VII and his consort Queen Alexandria were the first reigning monarchs to visit the town when they came ashore in 1902, shortly after Edward had succeeded to the throne. The brand new Royal Yacht

Dimond Street on the day of the Investiture of the Prince of Wales in 1911.

Victoria and Albert had sailed into the Haven on the evening of Friday 22 August and the following day the rumour had spread throughout the town that the King was on board and intended to land. This he duly did, a royal salute from the Defensible Barracks confirming the news for those who had not already rushed to the dockyard gates to welcome him and cheer.

The visit was unplanned and a hurried order had to be sent from the dockyard to town butcher Jack Elliot, ordering him to bring his carriage and horses for use by the royal party. Elliot drove the King to Pembroke where the party was escorted around Pembroke Castle and Monkton Priory before lunching at Brownslade, the home of Colonel and Lady Lambton. Thirty of the famous Castlemartin black cattle were shown to the King and Queen while they were at Brownslade and the party then headed off to Stack Rocks. The Dockyard Choir happened to be at the spot, on their annual outing, and duly sang the National Anthem for the royal visitors. Another choir party, this time from St Patrick's Church in Pennar, sang to the King when they drove to nearby St Govan's but, while Queen Alexandria went down the steep steps to see the church on the cliff bottom, the King stayed firmly in his carriage seat.

The return journey took the royal party through Pembroke, down Ferry Lane, up Dimond Street and Commercial Row and into the dockyard.

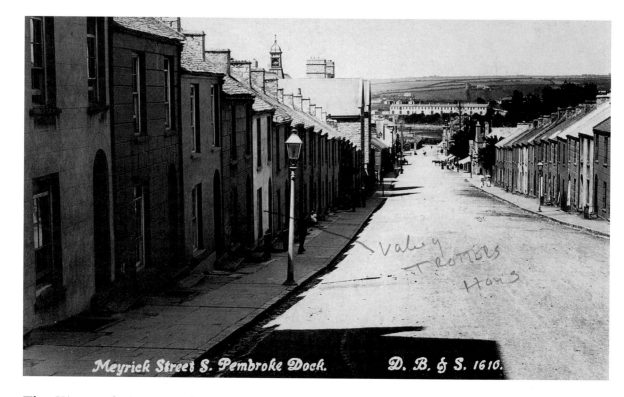

Meyrick Street S. Pembroke Dock.   D. B. & S. 1610.

The King and Queen re-boarded the *Victoria and Albert* and the next morning she sailed out of the Haven, bound for the Isle of Man. Pembroke Dock had to wait another 50 years for its next royal visit.

The coronations and deaths of kings and queens were celebrated or, at least, marked with dutiful regularity in the town. Queen Victoria's accession to the throne had been made public by a proclamation outside the dockyard gates in 1837. Her Jubilee, a celebration of 50 long and successful years on the throne, was celebrated on 21 June 1887. A procession, headed by the Loyal North Lancs Military Band, marched around the town, through the dockyard and up to the Barrack Hill. There, hundreds of spectators, children and church choirs sang the National Anthem and *God Bless the Prince of Wales* before the children dispersed to their various schoolrooms for tea. The Queen's Diamond Jubilee in 1897 was celebrated in much the same way as her Jubilee, ten years before – even though the Queen herself was long past caring about such things and was, by now, looking forward to nothing so much as a merciful release from her duties.

The actual occasion of Victoria's death on 22 January 1901 was observed with great sorrow in the town. The dockyard was closed, along with all the businesses and schools, and, as a mark of respect, an 81 gun salute was fired from the walls of the Defensible Barracks.

Meyrick Street at the beginning of the twentieth century. The military stables at Llanion can be seen at the bottom of the road.

While the coronation of King Edward VII was delayed because of his sudden attack of appendicitis, a decision was taken to proceed with the coronation festivities and these were duly held in the town on 26 June 1902. The day began with church services, when prayers were offered for the recovery of the new sovereign. Then followed processions – 3,500 children are said to have gathered together in Albion Square, each of them carrying a flag. An Historical Pageant and Empire Carnival were held and the day concluded with a concert in the market house.

The Investiture of the Prince of Wales in 1911 was marked with giant fleurs de lys above the dockyard gates and a gigantic bonfire on the Barrack Hill. The coronation of King George V took place that same year and was an excuse for yet more parades and bonfires.

Clearly the people of Pembroke Dock enjoyed a good state occasion, treating it as an excuse for a day's holiday or a party. In the days before formal drinking hours there is no doubt that the doors of the public houses would have been open all day long and liberal quantities of ale would have been consumed. At times it seemed as if any excuse for a celebration was eagerly seized on. Even the centenary of Robert Raikes, the founder of the Sunday School movement, was celebrated with great gusto on 28 June 1880; bands, marches and celebratory teas being the order of the day.

The Co-Op bread cart, complete with driver, outside the Bird in Hand public house in Lewis Street, circa 1910.

After Edward's visit in 1902, life in the dockyard town quickly got back to normal. It was a hard life, working in the yards, and so it is perhaps understandable if the men seized whatever chance they could get to 'take it easy' for a brief period.

The daily routine was nothing if not regular. Work usually began early, 7.00 a.m. in the summer, 7.30 a.m. in the winter, with dinner being taken between 12.00 and 1.30. The afternoon work session lasted until 5.30 p.m., the men finishing an hour earlier in winter. On Saturdays the work force was expected to work only until mid-day. Sunday was a day of rest with no work expected or done.

Some of the men who lived locally in the town of Pembroke Dock were able to get home during their 90 minute lunch break but many workers came from Pembroke or Monkton. Some even came from across the river, from villages such as Llangwm or Landshipping. Most of these men still came to work each day by rowing boat and for them there was no chance of going home for lunch. For them it was a case of a bottle of cold tea and sandwiches, either on some grassy spot within the yards or on the slopes of the Barrack Hill.

For a few years between 1882 and 1885 the wife of Captain Superintendent A.J.Chatfield organised and ran a soup kitchen in the yards. It was designed to provide those men who lived some distance away with a hot meal at

Queen Street in the early years of the twentieth century.

Bush Estate Offices, Pembroke Dock.

Bush Estate Office at the junction of Bush Hill and Ferry Lane. Bush House, home of the Meyrick family, principal landowners in the area, lay half a mile to the south.

mid-day and was funded by nominal contributions from the workforce and from the money collected at concerts Mrs Chatfield had organised. Each man apparently received one and a half pints of soup each day.

A tradition gradually developed within most Royal Dockyards that children would bring freshly prepared meals, hot and straight from the oven, to the dockyard gates for their fathers or brothers. This was undoubtedly done at Pembroke Dock for those workers who did not wish to make the trip home. The advent of compulsory schooling would have had some effect on this practice but it still continued for many years at Pembroke Dock and other yards with wives or older children who had left school being forced to carry the hot lunch to the dockyard gates.

Meanwhile the 'building blocks', so necessary for any community to grow and thrive were being gradually put into place. The town police station was built in Charlton Place in 1889. Before that, a house in Albion Square had been used as the police station but it was far from satisfactory. By the end of the century the establishment consisted of one Superintendent, one Sergeant and just seven constables, far fewer than the number of Metropolitan Police used to guard the gates and slipways of the dockyard.

The Pembroke Dock Co-operative Society was begun in April 1888 in a house on the corner of Bush Street. A fire destroyed much of the stock but the Connaught Rangers managed to bring their hoses to the scene and contain the blaze. A huge purpose built Co-op building was erected in Albion Square in 1892 – the building still stands although the Co-op itself has now long gone.

By the end of the nineteenth century almost everybody in the town of Pembroke Dock was connected with the dockyard in one way or another. If they did not work in the yards themselves they probably had relatives who did. Policemen, school teachers, clergymen, everybody came into contact with the dockyard at some stage of their working lives. If they were involved in commerce or trade, perhaps running a shop or retail outlet, they were undoubtedly still connected with the dockyard in some way, either supplying the yards themselves or offering services to the workmen, selling them groceries and food, clothes or cigarettes and tobacco. The infrastructure of the town was based around one industry and one industry alone – shipbuilding.

Pembroke Dock had been created to build ships and, at that stage, nobody dared contemplate what might happen if the town's reason for existence should ever be suddenly taken away.

CHAPTER NINE

The Glory Years

T HE SECOND HALF OF the nineteenth century and first few years of the twentieth were undoubtedly the 'glory years' for Pembroke Dock and its Royal Naval Dockyard. By 1875 most of the slipways were up and running, some of them being over 300 yards in length. The advantage of this was that it enabled launches to take place at almost any state of tide.

By this time the yards were full of workmen's shops for a wide range of craftsmen and artisans. The blacksmith's shop alone employed nearly 200 hands and the perpetual crash of hammers and hum of machinery pervaded the air. James Anderson Findlay wrote about the yards at this time:

> on all sides is heard the din, clang and clash of hammers and machinery forging and manufacturing the various kinds of heavy iron work now so requisite in the present advanced state of shipbuilding. Here, also, are three immense steam hammers, beneath whose ponderous heads ponderous masses of red hot iron are continually becoming subject to their will.

To the right of the building sheds stood a long, slender structure with the roof and huge portions of its sides made entirely out of glass. Known rather euphemistically as 'The Glass Shed', this was where boats were kept and repaired. It has been well recorded that Pembroke Dockyard was not a repair yard, concentrating only on the building of ships. However, some repair work must have been carried out, otherwise there would have been no purpose behind 'The Glass Shed'. We also have the story of HMS *Asp*, the haunted survey vessel. Her captain wrote that his vessel had come to Pembroke Dockyard specifically for the purpose of repair.

By the year 1900, with 2,500 men employed in the yards, the economy of the town and surrounding area seemed relatively secure. Compared with other jobs in the vicinity, wages were high. In 1899 the average weekly

wage of a skilled dockyard worker was around twenty-four shillings. In comparison, the average weekly wage for farm workers in the county of Pembrokeshire was just 15s. 10d. By the end of the century the dockyard at Pembroke Dock had become the single biggest employer of labour in Wales, easily outstripping the various coal mines and iron foundries in the eastern part of the country.

There was a danger, of course, in 'keeping all of your eggs in one basket', and the period between 1850 and the end of the century had not been without serious difficulties for the dockyard.

In 1860 the iron clad *Warrior* was launched from the yards of C.J. Mare on the Thames. The first iron clad vessel in the world – even though the French *Gloire* had been laid down earlier – this revolutionary new warship effectively made every other warship in the world obsolete overnight. It was the end of the wooden warship and for dockyards such as Pembroke Dock, places that had been designed to build those wooden ships that had for so many years been the backbone and the strength of the Royal Navy, there was a very real concern about the future. The 121-gun ship of the line *Howe* and the 50-gun *Aurora*, built in 1860 and 1861 respectively, were the last of their kind to leave Pembroke Dockyard.

There was, of course, another major difficulty. The *Warrior* had been built in a private dockyard – was this the way forward? people began to ask. Royal Naval yards had neither the skills nor the facilities to produce such ships. Were they even necessary? Commercial shipyards already existed in various parts of Britain, often adjacent or close to coal mines and iron works, where the workforces were well used to dealing with iron. Sometimes these yards even belonged to the iron masters who owned and ran the nearby foundries and iron works. Places like Pembroke Dockyard seemed to have none of the qualities now needed to survive. From being the most modern and up to date of British shipyards, Pembroke Dock had suddenly sunk to the bottom of the pile.

The yard lay many miles away from suitable iron works and such coal as was available locally was not good steam coal. The workforce was totally unskilled in building in metal and, like most skilled tradesmen, they did not want to deviate from their traditional styles and methods of work. The thirteen building slips in the yards had been created to allow wooden ships to season on the stocks but these were suddenly not necessary any longer. And then, of course, the old chestnut of Pembroke Dock's relative isolation rapidly became an important issue once more.

Transporting people and raw materials to the dockyard had always been a problem. When Captain Superintendent Thomas Sabine Pasley left the yards in 1854 he chose to go by boat rather than make the long and arduous journey by coach through the wilds of Wales. It was clearly the easiest way to make the trip to London. Pasley had commented, only a few years before, that the chief drawback to Pembroke Dock was 'getting to or from it'.

In the years after 1860 the Admiralty was immediately faced by several major dilemmas. Some of these were easily answered; others needed more careful pondering.

Firstly, in order to solve the problem of its obsolete ships, immediate commissions were given for as many iron clad vessels as it was possible to build, from yards right across the country. In all of the Royal Naval Dockyards the building situation was revised as designers scratched their heads and wondered how best to proceed. All wooden ships currently on the stocks were hastily re-designed with protective belts of armour being incorporated into their hulls. Four vessels like this were built at Pembroke Dock, the *Prince Consort*, launched on 26 June 1862, being the yard's first iron-clad ship.

In a period of rapid retrenchment the Admiralty next gave serious consideration to the future of its dockyards. A Royal Commission was established to look into the matter and for a while they seriously considered the possibility of closing the yards at Deptford, Woolwich, Sheerness and Pembroke Dock. In the end only Deptford and Woolwich were closed. They were inconveniently situated and, importantly, did not have sufficient space – because, rather than close its yards, the Admiralty had decided to expand. Philip MacDougall has commented:

> This double closure did not mean that new Royal Dockyards were unnecessary. It simply meant that future yards should be located in areas more suited to current naval needs. Indeed, the same decade which saw the closure of the two Thames-side yards also saw construction work begin on a new dockyard on Haulbowline Island in Cork Harbour, this being designed to provide additional facilities for ships operating in the Western Approaches.

Lord Clarence Paget, Secretary of the Admiralty at that time, was soon to state publicly that, as Chairman of the Royal Commission, he could not agree to the inclusion of Pembroke Dock among the list of yards to be closed down. Pembroke Dock was, he stated, 'a most important dockyard'. And yet his words have more than a hollow ring to them.

In reality Pembroke Dock had been saved from the axe by two important considerations. Firstly there was the coming of the railway.

The 1840s were the years of the great railway boom across Britain. New railway tracks were laid almost every week and hundreds of tiny railway companies were set up. Many of them did not last for long, either quickly filing for bankruptcy or being swallowed up by the larger and more financially viable companies. By 1852 the South Wales Railway Company had opened its line as far as Carmarthen, at that time the closest railway line to Pembroke Dock.

In due course the line was extended westwards to Clynderwen and then, eventually, in 1854, to Haverfordwest. On 15 April 1856 Isambard Kingdom Brunel's great railway reached its terminus at Neyland (New Milford). Situated directly across the river from Pembroke Dock this new railway link provided a useful means of transport for people going to and from the dockyard or, indeed, the town. However, it was not until several years later that the yards themselves were connected to the main railway system.

The Pembroke and Tenby Railway was begun in 1863, one of the main investors in the project being none other than David Davies of Llandinam, Wales's first millionaire and the guiding force behind the creation of Barry Docks. The first train between Tenby and the dockyard town steamed into the new Pembroke Dock station in August 1864. A banquet to celebrate the event, the significance of which was clear to all concerned, was held in the Victoria Hotel. A connection to the main line at Whitland was begun

APPLY TERRACE & STATION PEMBROKE DOCK.

The Great Western Railway took over the line between Tenby and Pembroke Dock in 1897. This shows Pembroke Dock station about 1902. From here a single line ran into the dockyard.

in 1865 and opened a year later. At long last Pembroke Dock had good communication to the outside world. When the Great Western Railway took over the line in 1896 they began a series of improvements such as extending and covering the station platform with a glazed roof and then extending the goods yard in nearby Water Street.

Soon after the railway arrived at Pembroke Dock, a single line was built from the station, initially situated at the end of Dimond Street, close to what soon became known as Apley Terrace, crossing several of the town streets as it snaked into the dockyard itself. Another extension was built along the shore and out along an embankment, to the south of Hobbs Point, called the New Pier. Henceforth the importing of goods and raw materials into the dockyard was made considerably easier and effectively eliminated one of the main concerns about the location of the yards.

The second saving grace for Pembroke Dockyard was the evolution of the composite warship. Composite ships were something of a compromise, being vessels that had wooden planking laid over iron frames, thus neatly combining traditional and modern warship design. It was the ideal medium for the gunboats and small craft of the Victorian gunboat era. In the words of Commander J. S. Guard:

> As far as Pembroke Dockyard was concerned this had the advantage of using its two most plentiful assets – the large stock of timber and the local shipwrights' skill in using it.

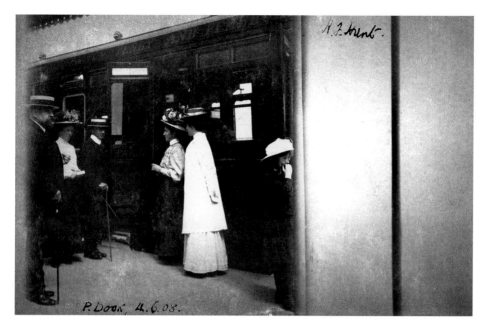

A rare view of the inside of Pembroke Dock station – elegance would seem to be the order of the day for these travellers.

A trap conveying passengers from the station to their destination in the town. Two horses are needed to cope with the heavy luggage.

Large numbers of small, shallow-draught gunboats would be required in the years ahead as the British Empire rapidly approached its 'high noon'. Many of these hurriedly built boats were soon flying the flag in distant corners of the world, defending outposts and areas of which the shipwrights at Pembroke Dock had never even heard. The yards quickly began to specialise in craft such as this but, with a wary eye to the future, they also began to train the craftsmen in the finer points of design and construction in iron and steel.

For the moment Pembroke Dockyard had been reprieved. Yet despite the new railway link, communication between the yards and London – indeed, to almost any part of the country – was still far from easy. The train journey to London still took nearly ten hours and in the years ahead this would prove to be an important consideration.

Rarely did a year pass between 1860 and 1900 without at least one ship being launched at Pembroke Dock. In 1889 there were six launches, four of them being composite gunboats, the other two being the 3rd class cruisers *Blanche* and *Blonde*. In January of the following year the yards built their last wooden ship. This was the Training Brig *Mayflower* that eased down the slipway on 20 January 1890. It must have been a moment of pure nostalgia for the shipwrights of the dockyard town and many of them could be excused for thinking that they had slipped back in time.

The covered building slips of Pembroke Dock were again proving useful during these years. Adapting the yards to modern technology was time consuming. There was also considerable debate about warship design in this period. As a result ships often stood for some time on the stocks before they were launched. Iron and steel were prone to rusting if left untreated in the open air for too long. At Pembroke Dockyard the partially built ships

HMS *Blonde*, a sleek scout cruiser launched on 22 June 1910. This view shows her moored against Carr Jetty soon after her launch.

H.M.S. BLONDE.

could nestle safely and happily under cover for as long as was needed.

By now, of course, the yards were heavily involved in the creation of some of the largest capital ships that had ever graced the navy. The *Empress of India*, a huge battleship armed with four 13.5 inch guns, was launched on 7 May 1891 while the *Repulse* entered the water the following year. On 8 May 1895 it was the turn of the *Renown*, the first British battleship with all-steel armour plating. These were gigantic and enormously powerful warships, the symbol of British sea power that was feared and respected throughout the world. As far as Pembroke Dock was concerned, the real wonder was how they were ever completed at all. The only fitting out berth that the yards possessed was the relatively tiny Hobbs Point and the installation of engines and masts into these magnificent ships from that jetty has to have been a miracle of engineering and improvisation.

Things were made somewhat easier by the opening of Carr Jetty at the beginning of the twentieth century, the long-awaited deep water fitting out berth for the yards. By now, however, it was clear that the dockyard simply was not big enough to cope with large vessels like the *Renown* and *Hannibal*. By the beginning of the twentieth century Pembroke Dock had become a cruiser yard. Not that it seemed to matter to the ordinary man in the street. There were few qualms about the future.

Pembroke Dock was secure in its own little island of prosperity. The people of the town knew that they were different from the rest of the county and life was settled and prosperous with most people in government employment. The wages may not have been brilliant but they were adequate and, perhaps equally as important, the work was permanent and pensionable.

The town of Pembroke Dock was full of well-stocked shops and the municipal functions of the community were catered for by the elected officers of Pembroke Borough. In the years after the formation of the town the people of the new community had acted, largely, for themselves in municipal matters. However, the year after the Municipal Act of 1835, the town became a ward of Pembroke Borough, known as Pater Ward. Mayors of the Borough were elected annually, the first Pembroke Dock man to fill the post being Captain James Cocks who took up his position in November 1860.

The foundation stone of a Mechanics' Institute was laid in Dimond Street on 27 June 1862. The Institute had its beginnings in a house in Lewis Street, two dockyard officers founding the organisation to help young men of the town, in 1850. The new premises were built on land

Bush Street seems relatively quiet the day this photograph was taken. The canopy on the left gives shade to the shop and business premises of S. J. Allen, the renowned local photographer.

donated by the Meyrick family, the lease being granted for 99 years at an annual rent of half a crown. Soon the new Institute had a library of over 3,500 books, a billiards room and a reading room, all available to people of the town for an annual subscription of six shillings.

The first bank in the town was the Milford Haven Bank, situated in Commercial Row. It later became a branch of the London and Provincial Bank, its premises being located on the north-west corner of Dimond Street. The National and Provincial Bank also arrived at this time, locating itself in premises in Meyrick Street. By the end of the nineteenth century Barclays and Lloyds had established their branches in the town, Barclays occupying the position of honour on the corner of Dimond Street and Meyrick Street.

Many of the workmen who came to the dockyard were staunch nonconformists – many of them were also strongly in favour of the temperance movement. Following the appearance in the town of a noted temperance orator called Scott in about 1845, many people joined the ranks of total abstainers. As a result, a Temperance Hall was built on the corner of Dimond Street and Lewis Street. In an act of incredible generosity, the mortgage for the building was paid off by William Griffiths in 1868 and the Hall donated to the Temperance Society. Primarily intended for temperance meetings only, the building was soon being used for many different functions. It continued in use until destroyed by German bombs in the Second World War. The Pater Hall was then erected in its place on the same site in 1957.

Almost from the beginning, the religious and spiritual needs of townspeople were well catered for. However, it was not until thirty years after the town's inception that a church was built in the town, members of the orthodox religion having to travel two miles into nearby Pembroke if they wished to attend services. The original idea was to build a church on the old town burial ground but this was finally dropped and the Meyrick family of nearby Bush House donated a suitable piece of land close to the town centre. St Johns was then built in Bush Street between 1845 and 1848 and, with the consecration of the church by the Bishop of St David's on 29 September 1848, Pembroke Dock duly became a new parish.

Pembroke Street, circa 1860, with the north western gun tower and the Haven beyond.

The Bazaar, Pembroke St., Pembroke Dock.

The premises of town photographer Morgan housed not only his studio but also his stock of books and stationary. It was also the local branch of the Society for the Promotion of Christian Knowledge.

J. EASTLAKE. THOMAS.

J. E. Thomas, 32, Bush Street, Pembroke Dock.

Another shop front postcard, this view shows the premises of J Eastlake Thomas, local butcher.

Prior to the opening of the church, services had been held, for a few years, in one of the classrooms of the National School. The foundation stone of the new church was laid by Lord Aukland, then First Lord of the Admiralty, and inside the present church are several interesting mural tablets. The most fascinating, but also most mysterious, reads:

In Memory of
Lewis Davies
Who was killed in an attack on pirates
On the coast of Borneo
On the 7th Sept 1868.
Aged 21 years and 8 months.
This tablet is erected by his shipmates.

Quite who the unfortunate Lewis Davies was, and the reason for his memorial tablet in St Johns, may never be known but it certainly catches the mood of the time and makes fascinating reading.

St Patrick's Church in Treowen Road in Pennar was built in 1893–95, the organ for the church having been taken from St John's. It was intended to provide a place of worship for people in the Pennar, Lower Pennar and

St John's Church, Pembroke Dock.

St John's Church in Bush Street, built between 1845 and 1848, was the first new church in south west Wales built to Ecclesiastical principles.

St. Patrick's Church, Pennar, Pembroke Dock.

St Patrick's Church in Pennar was built between 1893 and 1895 to take the overflow from St John's.

Bufferland areas of the town and had replaced the small wooden mission cottage that had previously served as a base in Pennar. St Teilo's Church was located in London Road at Waterloo and was built in 1903 by J. Coates Carter. An old turnpike had once existed close to the church, at nearby Bierspool, but it had long gone by the year 1903.

The first chapel in Pembroke Dock was Bethany, set high up on the ridge at the top of Tregenna's Hill. The original building was erected in 1818 on land donated by Sir John Owen of Orielton and was surrounded by a stone wall some seven feet in height. Inside the wall was a burial ground where many of the town's earliest inhabitants were laid to rest. The foundation stone of the present building was laid by Rose Reed, the daughter of Sir Edward Reed, in 1877, just before the launch of the Japanese corvette *Hei-Yei* which was built at the nearby private yard of Jacobs Pill.

Other chapels in the town include Bethel (1873–75), St Andrews (1865–66), Trinity (1851–52) and Gilgal in Pennar (1862). Tabernacle Wesleyan Chapel was built in Meyrick Street between 1846 and 1848. Methodism had strong links with the area, John Wesley himself having visited Pembrokeshire several times between 1767 and 1769. Tabernacle was, and still remains, the largest chapel west of Swansea although it has now been changed to the Zion Free Church.

In the early days of the town there were few followers of the Roman Catholic faith in the town. Those that did live there met for worship in a house in King Street. The first Catholic priest to live in the town was Father Lewis who regularly preached in the open air, from the slopes of the hill above Pembroke Street. Largely due to his efforts, as the Catholic population of the town gradually increased, St Mary's Church was built at the top end of North Meyrick Street between 1846 and 1847.

The town's new burial ground was opened on London Road at Waterloo in 1869 as the old cemetery in Park Street had already become too full. The new cemetery had considerable open ground on which to expand.

The Salvation Army came to the town in January 1883, the first Captain being a man called Henry Gover. General Booth, the founder of the

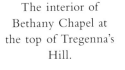

The interior of Bethany Chapel at the top of Tregenna's Hill.

Bethel Chapel, built between 1873 and 1875.

Wesley Chapel, still the largest non-conformist meeting house west of Swansea.

Salvation Army, visited the town on 1 May 1883 and spoke in Albion Square Chapel. The building was crowded with people eager to hear the famous man speak and many failed to gain admission. In a town as rough and tough as Pembroke Dock there is no doubt that the services of the Salvation Army were frequently called upon and well used in these last years of Queen Victoria's reign.

The Pembroke Dock Salvation Army Band.

The dockyard fire brigade, complete with fire engine, pose for this photograph. Most of the firemen were serving members of the Dockyard Police, hence the uniforms.

A volunteer fire brigade was formed in the town in 1897 but it lasted only a few years before being disbanded through lack of interest and fire fighting duties were taken over by the Dockyard Police. This was not dissimilar to many other towns where, until after the Second World War, most police forces offered a similar service. An Auxiliary Fire Brigade was formed in the town in the twentieth century, remaining a voluntary unit until after the war.

St Teilo's Church, situated on London Road, close to the Commercial Inn. The architect was J Coates Carter.

This faded photograph by Charles Allen of Tenby shows assembled dignitaries for the launch of the Japanese corvette *Hi Yei*, built at Jacobs Pill and launched on 12 June 1877. By 1885 the private dockyard had gone into liquidation.

Modern visitors and readers might be excused for thinking that the only shipbuilding in Pembroke Dock was linked to the Royal Naval Dockyard. Not so! There were a number of private shipyards located around the town during the nineteenth century, notably Robertson's in Front Street. These yards built two beautiful and well-known barques called the *Resolution* and *Cambria*, the former being wrecked while carrying timber from America. In February 1888 Messrs J. and W. Francis also began a shipbuilding business in Front Street, the yards continuing to operate up until the Great War.

The mould loft of Jacobs Pill was later converted into use as an isolation hospital for the town.

Little now remains of Jacobs Pill dockyard on Pembroke River, just a few old walls and this rusted gate pin.

Richard Allen and James Warlow formed a small shipbuilding company in the town in the 1850s, building a vessel called the *Arethusa* on the west side of Water Street. They also built the 1,250-ton *Carmarthenshire* which was supposedly the first merchant ship to enter Yokohama harbour. The company went out of business in 1868, but Allen later formed several other companies, notably Richard Allen & Sons who won the contract to repair lightships for Trinity House.

Water Street, Pembroke Dock.

The best remembered private yard from these years was Jacobs Pill in Pennar. Founded by Sir Edward Reed, one time Chief Constructor for the Admiralty and later MP for Pembroke Borough, Jacobs Pill stood on the banks of the Pembroke River and was run by the Milford Haven Shipbuilding and Engineering Company. Reed was chairman of the company and a prime mover in all that it set out to achieve.

Through Reed's influence an order was obtained to build a corvette for the Japanese navy. The ship was launched on 12 July 1877 and His Excellency Jushie Wooyeno Kagenori, Envoy Extraordinary and Minister Plenipotentiary to the Mikado of Japan came to the town to witness the event. A large procession greeted the Envoy at the station and escorted him to Jacobs Pill where the christening ceremony was performed by Reed's daughter and, accompanied by the music of three bands, the *Hei-Yei* slipped easily into the waters of Pembroke River. The *Hei-Yei* was an armoured corvette armed with three 17cm and six 15cm breech loading guns. She was the first armoured ship in the Japanese navy and later saw service in the Sino-Japanese War, being badly damaged at the Battle of the Yellow Sea.

The launching party, a renowned and distinguished group that included guests such as Admiral Lord Clarence Paget, then attended a grand cele-bratory banquet at the Victoria Hotel. The day finished with a firework

Water Street, one of the important arterial roads that led to London Road and the route to the east.

display on the slopes of the Barrack Hill. Sadly, Jacobs Pill built only a few more vessels, including one called *Acorn* for the Admiralty, but by 1884 the yards had closed down. At this distance in time it is worth considering the influence and actions of Sir Edward Reed. In furthering his dockyard he used his position and contacts quite unashamedly. These days the man would probably be arrested!

Mrs Peters, in *The History of Pembroke Dock*, recounts a story about an earthquake in the town:

> The earthquakes which disturbed the inhabitants of the town about twelve years ago will be easily remembered by many. The first happened about midnight on Wednesday 17 August 1892; other and slighter shocks were felt about six weeks later. Although, perhaps, not very terrorizing to people who have been in lands where earthquakes are not infrequent, the first unwelcome visitant to our peaceful little corner of the Principality was sufficiently alarming to cause many to rise from their beds and go into the streets.

Whether the disturbances really were earthquakes will never be known as there were not the means of recording or checking that exist now. Perhaps, just perhaps, the shaking was caused by the submarine mining experiments that were being carried out at Pennar.

At the time, however, it seemed that not even the natural forces of the universe, the planets or even the earth itself could knock Pembroke Dock from its equilibrium.

CHAPTER TEN

Work Hard, Play Hard

As we have already seen, the life of a dockyard worker was never an easy one. The hours were long and the work grindingly hard. In the early days of the yards all building was carried out in the open air and men often worked knee-deep in mud and slime, totally vulnerable to the wind and rain. After mechanisation came to the yards in the years after 1860, the noise and heat would have been nigh on unbearable. The sheer physical labour of the tasks would have killed off, or damaged for life, many modern workers.

So it was understandable that some dockyard workers looked for easy ways out, the odd stolen five minutes when the charge hand wasn't looking or the long, slow shuffle to the next job. Yet it would be wrong to view all dockyard maties as idle skivers. Most of them were hard working and proud of their reputations as skilled hands. The Pembroke Dock workforce was a close-knit community and, as you might expect in such a small town, many of them were related to each other. It was not unusual to find whole gangs of shipwrights made up of brothers, uncles and cousins. Going into the dockyard to work was clearly a family affair.

Leisure time was limited but it was important. Much of it was closely linked to the twin organisations of any Welsh town – the chapels and the pubs.

For many years the chapels and churches of the town were also the centre of social activity for most of the population. Quite apart from attendance at service on a Sunday, they would offer prayer meetings, Band of Hope, youth clubs and discussion groups. Concerts were held on a regular basis and every place of worship had an excellent, well-rehearsed choir ready and able to sing at a moment's notice. Many of them would travel all over the county, competing in one of the Eisteddfodiau that were held by chapels from the various villages and towns.

A hunt meeting gathers outside Llanion Barracks, around about 1910. Despite its industrial base, the gentry of the area, plus army officers and dockyard officials, often enjoyed country pastimes like hunting and shooting.

Christmas Eve was always a popular time and every religious denomination had its own party of singers who would spend the evening carolling in the town. In those days it was unlikely to be money that they were rewarded with – coffee and Christmas cake were much more likely to be dispensed. Mrs Peters tells of one custom that had been strong in the 1850s and 1860s but which, by the end of the century had virtually disappeared from the streets of the town – the guisers:

> If seen at all now, they are only a group of boys dressed up in women's garments and singing a few snatches of the latest comic songs; but the 'guisers' of those past days were a different thing. Then the lads, with blackened visages, grotesque masks, and a curious song, were indeed very amusing. Probably this 'guising' was a survival of the mimicry and masques of the mummers who took such an essential part in the Christmas ceremonials of the Tudor period.

The original guisers would, when rewarded with a coin, act out a sketch or small play that involved Father Christmas challenging a Turkish knight, the defeat of the infidel and his treatment and cure by a doctor with the following words:

> I've got a little bottle
> In my inside pocket,
> Called Okum Pokum Elecampane:
> Rise up dead man and fight again.

Many of the chapels, in particular, were heavily involved with the temperance movement, hence the particularly large number of Bands of Hope in the town. Gilgal Chapel in Pennar always saw itself as something of an enemy of the heavy drinker. The chapel would not have anyone in its fellowship who was involved with the selling of alcohol and frowned on anybody who spent too much time in local pubs like the *Alma* or the *Kilwendege*. As if to prove the point no fewer than 50 people 'signed the pledge' to become total abstainers during a temperance meeting in Pennar during the 1860s. To find that level of support for abstention in a dockyard town was, to say the least, unusual.

The Borough of Pembroke is reputed to have had over 200 public houses at one stage – they would all have been required to help slake the thirst of the dockyard workers after their shifts in the yards. Many of the smaller pubs would be run by men who, during the day, worked in the dockyard. As they were government employees, however, they were not able to put their names above the doors. Many of the early beer houses were, there-fore, run by workers' wives or daughters. In the 1860s the Commercial Inn in Pembroke Street – one of several Pembroke Dock pubs of the same name – was governed by Mary Brown, although the real landlord was her father Edward. As he worked in the yards he was supposedly disqualified from keeping a public house. There are many more examples of similar arrangements in the town.

The names of many famous men are connected with or linked to the pubs of Pembroke Dock. One memorable night at the end of the century saw the officers of HMS *Monarch* hold open house in the Bush Hotel. Included in the party was Lieutenant Robert Falcon Scott, a man who later went on to immortality with his failed attempt at reaching the South Pole, and a certain Lieutenant Dickens, grandson of the famous novelist. Arthur Orton, the famous Tichborne Claimant, once stayed at the Commercial Inn (now the Flying Boat). Local legend declares that he left without paying his bill! Several public houses in town claim an acquaintance with the future General Gordon while the Bush Hotel once played host to Lord Rosebery, the Prime Minister, and Prince Louis of Battenberg.

The atmosphere in these old taverns can, now, only be imagined but, at the end of a working day, they would have been filled with brawny riggers and shipwrights, soldiers from the Barracks and people from the town trying to relax for a few hours after a day of back-breaking work. Floors would have been liberally strewn with sawdust and, behind the bar, there would have been clay pipes and cheap cigars for sale. The rooms would have reeked with the fumes of beer and tobacco. H. H. R. Reynolds wrote a small booklet, *Some Old Inns and Reminiscences of Pembroke Dock*, in the years just before the Second World War and in that publication he tried to capture a little of the mood of the town and the leisure activities of its people:

As beer and tobacco generally go together many of the old generation will remember Miss Poyers' shop in Dimond Street. Red Stamp Tobacco [was] kept in jars in the window and snuff kept in a bladder ... and tobacco out of old jars seemed to have been a luxury for some folk ... Edward Jacques, Wrights Cut, Cavendish, Irish Twist and Bird's Eye.

The Pier Hotel stood in London Road for many years but was destroyed by German bombs during the Second World War.

Smoking, then, would have been commonplace. Nobody had the slightest idea of the dangers of tobacco and all men would have carried a pipe or rolled their own cigarettes. It seems strange now to think of smoking as a leisure activity, but for the people of Victorian Pembroke Dock that was exactly what it was. The better class of hotels and taverns in the town regularly advertised their smoking rooms, actively encouraging visitors to come and try them out.

Smoking was just one of many activities that the workmen of the town enjoyed. Some of their activities and pastimes now seem unusual, particularly to supposedly more sophisticated twenty-first-century eyes. There was no television or radio in those days and many of the men's leisure activities had a distinctly 'home made' feel to them.

Marbles was always a popular game for the dockyard workers. It was usually played after work at the bottom of the Avenue, the wide road leading down from the lower slopes of the Barrack Hill and finishing at the dockyard gates. A large ring would be formed, schoolboys and casual passers-by being included amongst the eager spectators, and the game played out with great skill and excited catcalls from participants and watchers alike.

This view of Laws Street shows the Bush Hotel, once one of the main licensed premises in the town.

Dimond Street, Pembroke Dock.

The Royal
Edinburgh Hotel,
complete with ornate
canopy over the
entrance door, is
shown here in all its
glory.

Knapon was another popular game for some years. It was presumably some form of the old Welsh game of Cnapan, or at least a derivation from it, and appears to have been a sport that can be best described as a combination of street hockey, football and the Eton Wall Game! Shrove Tuesday was always the great day for the game when dozens, if not hundreds, of players took part. Knapon was later outlawed by the dockyard officials as it was considered too dangerous and far too many of the workforce were calling in sick after playing the game.

Industrial injuries were another matter. The risk of physical injury was always high, most dockyards having a long list of serious accidents. Deaths were not uncommon and Pembroke Dockyard was no different in that respect. After the introduction of iron and steel to the building process in the years after 1860 the rate of industrial injury increased significantly. Falls from gantries and staging had always been a major problem. Now, added to these, came the risk of serious burns as metal was heated to immense temperatures. There was also the risk of injury from shards of flying metal and, most terrifying of all, of limbs becoming trapped in heavy machinery. Lawrence Phillips quotes the example of William Williams who:

had been greasing cogs in a machine in No. 2 Fitters Shop on the morning of 21st May 1900 when he was caught in the machinery. He

Victoria Road at
the bottom of the
Barrack Hill.

was taken to the Surgery with a fractured skull and his right hand amputated 'all except the thumb'.

Williams died the following day, his widow receiving £193 14*s*. 11*d*. in compensation. He was just one of many who met their deaths in the dockyard. And his family had to pay for the cost of his coffin. Most workers paid two pence each week as an insurance against any funeral costs – in those days it was a wise precaution.

One of the many tasks of the Dockyard Surgeon was to visit those men who were injured in work or had fallen sick. At potato picking time – Pembrokeshire 'earlies' having been an important part of the economy of the area for many years – there was often a long sick list as men either harvested their own small crops or, if they were lucky enough to be in the right place at the right time, hired themselves out to local farmers to earn a little extra money. The image of supposedly sick dockyard maties dropping their buckets and running for the nearest hedge when they heard the steady clip-clop of the surgeon's horse coming up the lane remains something to conjure – naughty schoolboys indeed!

Other supposedly dangerous games played by dockyard men were tipcat and catty, although quite what they entailed has now been long forgotten.

Presumably they were some type of chase game. Tipcat and catty were also frowned on by dockyard authorities and discouraged whenever possible. A more acceptable pastime in the last years of the nineteenth century was the strange game of Lead Birds.

Lead Birds involved the images of birds, camels or elephants being made from a chalk mould. These were then placed on the ground and small chunks of lead were thrown at them. Each of the objects had a set value and it took so many hits for the object to become the property of the other player. Despite its seemingly innocent nature, the game was said to have led to many fights between players as tempers and enthusiasm invariably ran high.

Horse and pony races were held on the top of the Barrack Hill on several occasions in the early years of the town, all classes of society within the new community attending and betting on the outcome of the various races. Once the Defensible Barracks were built this practice was ended and horse fanciers had to make do with steeplechase meetings in the country areas around the town.

Gambling, however, continued. In one well-recorded instance the landlord of the Railway Hotel, a Scot by the name of Walter Borroman,

refereed a foot race between two of his more 'well endowed' customers, both of whom weighed in at more than 19 stone. The race was for a wager of £5 and was reportedly won by Mr Sloggett. The race was not the only time Mr Sloggett was to appear in the town's history. H. H. R. Reynolds refers to him in the Bush Tavern when:

> During a heated argument the great Tom Sayers, it was stated, was knocked down by Mr Sloggett, a local resident.

Sadly Reynolds does not go on to say what caused Mr Sloggett to hit the great bare-fist fighter and the origins of the story have now been lost.

Holiday outings were important, particularly in the days when long vacations and weekends away were unheard of. Holidays with pay were not general in Britain until after the Second World War; even Bank Holidays did not become part of the British social scene until the 1880s. However, day trips – perhaps on Sundays or once Bank Holidays became established – were an important part of life in the town.

Whit Monday excursions were usually taken to places like Stack Rocks and St Govan's Chapel, although Begelly Common seems to have been a popular spot for many years. People rode in carts or on bicycle or, if there was no other way, they made the journey on foot. Walking was far more

The Albion Square complex was built in the 1830s and soon became a central focus for the town. The building on the right, Albion Square School, opened on 20 December 1877.

A victorious darts team from the town, complete with trophy.

For many years the easiest way to travel around the town and immediate area was by bus. This shows a Silcox double decker, a famous sight in the town, in Albion Square and dates from 1949. In the years after the Second World War the Silcox company established something of a monopoly on bus travel in south Pembrokeshire.

common in the nineteenth century. There are recorded instances of men having to walk six or seven miles into work each day and thinking next to nothing about it. So to walk to Freshwater East, Angle or Broadhaven for a day's outing was nothing unusual.

Very often trips were organised by the chapels and Sunday Schools. The Sunday School outing, of course, has become famous in British folklore,

An athletics competition in the town park, this post card dates to 1917. The message on the back reads 'This photo is of yours truly which, I know, will be of interest to you.' Notice, there is no crash mat or sand pit for the high jumper to land in.

Pembroke Dock was only connected to the main railway system in August 1864. It gave new life to the dockyard and to the leisure options for dockyard workers – now they could take day trips to places like nearby Tenby. This view shows a tank engine emerging from Golden Hill tunnel between Pembroke and Pembroke Dock.

children looking forward to the event for weeks before it actually took place and all dutifully attending every Sunday in order to gain their mark and qualify for inclusion on the trip. Such outings usually took place around Whitsun time. In the days before charabancs the children were transported in carts behind panting farm horses, singing and laughing all the way to the beach. After a day on the sands they would be treated to tea and then, tired and half asleep, it was time for the journey back to the dockyard town.

June 28 was Victorian Coronation Day, when everyone celebrated the accession of Queen Victoria to the throne. Being a 'government' town it was a recognised dockyard holiday and on that day, in particular, semi-rustic sports and, in later years, bicycle races were held. For many years an annual sports meeting was held on a stretch of ground close to London Road. All types of athletic events were staged, events even extending to donkey races, but for the boys of the town it was sliding on the watery meadow land that provided most fun.

Organised sports clubs were created in the town right from the beginning. Many of the churches and chapels formed tennis clubs and there were also courts in the dockyard, in Llanion Barracks and at the Royal Engineers Barracks at Pennar. Boxing had always been popular in the British army and so it was inevitable that the sport should become accepted in the town. Jimmy Wilde, the World Flyweight Champion, was a regular visitor and even fought in the town when he topped the bill in an Inter-Services Tournament in 1917. When, on 10 November 1917, the third garrison boxing tournament was held in the Market Hall there was an audience of nearly 4000 people to watch the contests.

Rugby had been played in Pembrokeshire since 1870 and the Pembroke Dock Rugby Club was founded in 1880. Their first game was played on the Barrack Hill, the club becoming affiliated to the Welsh Rugby Union in 1896. They took the name Pembroke Dock Harlequins in 1900 and still play under that name. Being able to call on players from the dockyard and the various army regiments stationed in the town – although the army also

Being located on the Milford Haven waterway, regattas were held on a regular basis in the town. This photograph shows Pennar Regatta, the event taking place close to the spot where a ferry boat disaster occurred in 1889. The boatman and 14 women passengers were drowned when the ferry boat capsized.

ran their own teams for many years – the Quins became a highly successful outfit, winning the Knock-out Cup for the first time in 1911 and their first ever Pembrokeshire Championship in 1913–14. For many years the club had its headquarters in the Royal Edinburgh Hotel. The club has produced many famous players, none more so than the legendary Ernie Finch who scored a spectacular try for Llanelli against the visiting New Zealand All Blacks in 1925 and went on to win several Welsh caps.

Pembroke Dock was fielding an Association Football team from the mid 1890s but the Dockyard Apprentices side was also renowned in the county for many years. Welsh League Football came to the area in the mid 1920s, the town side being placed in the first division. Despite leaving the League, once the dockyard closed, soccer continued to thrive in the town and Pembroke Borough joined the League in 1945, winning the Championship and the Cup in 1954–55 when players like Frankie Donovan and Billy Reed reigned supreme. Only in the final years of the twentieth century did the Borough finally put up the shutters and their famous ground on London Road has now been redeveloped for housing.

As the town was virtually enclosed by water on three sides it was inevitable that boating and sailing should play an important part in the leisure activities of many people. The wealthier citizens took to yachting, the working classes bought or built rowing boats that were used for fishing in the estuary. Regattas were popular, the two best known being held

The training ship Foudroyant *was moored for a while in the Haven off Pembroke Dock, the young trainees often coming ashore to take part in local activities.*

for many years at Front Street and off the ridge in Lower Pennar. These were water based sports and included events such as rowing, sculling, pole fighting and swimming.

For a number of years the training ship *Foudroyant* was moored off the town. Owned by J. R. Cobb, who also restored much of nearby Pembroke Castle, and later by his son Geoffrey, the *Foudroyant* was Nelson's flagship in the Mediterranean between 1789 and 1801. The Admiral regularly entertained Lady Hamilton in the great stern cabin of the ship and their illegitimate daughter was actually conceived there.

Sold out of the navy during Queen Victoria's reign, Cobb bought the ship and inaugurated her as a training vessel in 1896. The plan was for her to be sailed around the coast of Britain, giving the young trainees on board valuable experience of the sea while, by opening her up for visitors at the various ports she visited, the famous ship was also expected to make money for Mr Cobb. Unfortunately, the ship was wrecked on Blackpool sands in 1897 and Cobb was forced to buy a new vessel. This was the Indian-built *Trincomalee*. Her name was changed to *Foudroyant* and this was the vessel that came to Pembroke Dock. She was moored off the town between June 1904 and May 1905, the young trainees taking part in the Front Street Regatta during this time. She later returned to the area in 1930 when she was berthed at nearby Cosheston. The *Foudroyant* has recently been restored to her former glory and remains the oldest wooden ship still afloat.

An express train leaves Pembroke Dock station.

Pembroke Dock's first theatre was a portable one, known as Fenton's. It was located close to the Market Place and was patronised by many of the leading people in the town. In the 1850s Ord's Theatre stood at the top of Gwyther Street, regularly offering entertainment to the population. In addition, the town was regularly visited by travelling shows and theatre companies.

Queen's Theatre was built in Queen Street at the end of the nineteenth century, being managed first by Walter Canton and then by Tom Barger. Barger came from Liverpool and spent 30 years working in the music halls where he was renowned as a female impersonator, quick change artist and ventriloquist. For several years he ran the Commercial pub before taking over the Queen's. He later turned the theatre into a roller skating rink and, in the early twentieth century, the old place became White's Picture Palace, the first movie house in the town. Closed in the middle of the twentieth century, the theatre was reopened for a brief period in the 1980s after the Grand Cinema at the bottom of Meyrick Street – for so long a staple of entertainment for Pembroke Dock people – had closed its doors for the last time.

The town was well frequented by travelling fairs and the occasional circus. However, the best remembered of all the visiting attractions were the famous Buffalo Bill and his Wild West Show who came to Pembroke Dock on 14 May 1904. The spectacle of magnificently dressed American Indians, the US 7th Cavalry and a group of Cossack horsemen delighted the people of the town. It was something way beyond their understanding,

Pembroke Dock Market Hall. Notice the poster advertising the imminent arrival of Buffalo Bill's Wild West Show. The visit caused great excitement in the town and immediate neighbourhood.

S.J. Allen, seated centre, complete with family – wife, daughters, son-in-law. Most of the early photographs of the town come courtesy of Allen's all-seeing camera.

but they still marvelled at the display of horsemanship and trick shooting from Buffalo Bill Cody and his showmen.

During the last years of the nineteenth century and first two dozen years of the twentieth, the photographer S.J. Allen was busy recording the town's history on photograph and postcard. Born in Staffordshire, Allen moved to Tenby with his father, the early photographer Charles Smith Allen, when he was still a boy. Fascinated by the photographer's art, S.J. Allen opened his own studio in Pembroke Dock sometime in the early 1880s and, for a photographic pioneer like him, it was the ideal time to be starting a new business. Working out of his shop and studio at 26 Bush Street, his cards of launches, marches and street scenes in the town soon began to flood the market.

S.J. Allen was also an Alderman of the Borough of Pembroke and served as the Town Mayor between 1896 and 1897 when, during the celebrations for the Queen's Diamond Jubilee, he and his wife were presented to Victoria along with the mayors from all the other towns across the country. In 1897 it was his personal intervention with Austen Chamberlain, Civil Lord of the Admiralty, that prevented the closure of Hobbs Point, the town's main ferry point. Owned by the Admiralty, public access to the jetty – which was also the dockyard fitting out berth – had always been something of a thorny problem. S.J. Allen's intervention effectively gave the jetty to the people of the town in perpetuity. Allen died in 1926 but the family business continued for many years, only winding up in the mid-1960s.

Allen was not the only Pembroke Dock photographer of note. A man called Morgan (Christian name unknown) lived and worked in Pembroke Street at the same time as Allen was establishing his studios a few hundred yards away. The Nutshell Press in Queen Street was also producing fine postcard views of the town so that proud workmen and their families could collect, like thousands of other Victorians, photographic views of their home town and the surrounding area.

One of Pembroke Dock's famous ferry boats, approaching the Hobbs Point Jetty.

The procession to celebrate the King's coronation in 1911 moves steadily up Pembroke Street towards the Barrack Hill.

Hobbs Point was the main ferry jetty for the town but boats ran from several locations around the town, taking passengers to places such as Neyland and Burton across the Cleddau River. The Hard in Front Street had been built by the Admiralty for the town in 1827 and was particularly well used by market traders from the north of the county who regularly unloaded their wares across the beach. As far as they were concerned the great advantage of the Hard was that they did not have to pay to use it.

However, Hobbs Point was always the most popular and successful ferry boat base in the town. At one stage, in the days before Pembroke Dock had its own railway link, ferries ran every fifteen minutes from here to the pontoon at Neyland in order to connect with Brunel's railway. Even after Pembroke Dock station was opened, the ferries continued to run. In 1875 the fare was just 2d. single, 3d. return.

The Pembroke Dock and Neyland ferry boats were familiar and reassuring sights around the Haven and, over the years, vessels such as the *Amy*, the *Pioneer* and the *Menai* became part of the town history. The most popular of all the ferry boats, however, were the *Alumchine* and *Lady Magdalene* which arrived on the river in 1933. Replaced, in due course, by the *Cleddau King* and *Cleddau Queen*, the old boats were an important part of the Pembroke Dock social scene, allowing people access to the other side of the river and to places like Milford and Haverfordwest.

For many years a small ferry ran between Lower Pennar and Bentlass on the southern side of Pembroke River. Owned and operated by a boatman called Jones, the ferry offered easy access and transport across the river for dockyard workers who lived in the villages around Pembroke and Monkton. Unfortunately, the crossing was the scene of a major disaster on the afternoon of Friday 8 February 1889.

It was market day in Pembroke Dock and, as was the custom, several women took Mr Jones's ferry across the river in order to do their weekly shopping. The weather was quite stormy when the 14 women returned to the crossing point late in the afternoon. The boat was heavily laden with provisions and, amongst other things, sacks of flour. When water came slopping in over the side one of the women panicked and leapt to her feet. The boat was immediately overwhelmed by the tide and all the passengers, as well as Mr Jones and the boy assisting him, were drowned. The small boat went down only a few yards from the southern bank of the river but such was the ferocity of the waves and tide that there was no possibility of rescue.

A few years later Pembroke Dock workmen were involved in dramatic salvage operations off the island of Lundy. The battleship *Montagu* ran ashore on Shutter Point at the south-west corner of the island in a thick fog on the night of 30 May 1906. The tide swung the giant vessel broadside on to the rocks, both propellers were lost and a huge hole ripped in her bottom.

Salvage operations took many months, dozens of dockyard maties being taken out from Pembroke Dock on the tugs *Alligator* and *Volcano* to work on the wreck. The original plan was to seal off part of the ship, create a false bottom, force air into the sealed-up hull and float her off. The sharp rocks of Shutter Point held her fast, however, and the scheme was abandoned.

Work on the wreck was continually hampered by bad weather. On 1 August conditions were so bad that 63 of the dockyard workers refused to go on board the stranded vessel when they were mustered in the morning. Eventually, the *Montagu* had to be abandoned and she was officially 'paid off' on 20 August. The news was greeted with wild enthusiasm by the Pembroke Dock men. They had been putting in long days on the stricken vessel, some of their shifts lasting for up to thirty hours at a time. When Admiral Wilson, the man in charge of the salvage operations, broke the news, the Pembroke Dock maties celebrated by breaking into the works canteen – the only unlicensed inn in England as H.H.R.Reynolds, who visited the island with photographer S.J.Allen, recorded. The men helped themselves to the beer and several drank so much that they sustained serious injuries after slipping, totally intoxicated, down the cliffs and gullies of the island.

The year 1914 marked the centenary of Pembroke Dockyard and of the town. In order to commemorate the occasion a memorial was erected in Albion Square and the following words engraved upon the plinth:

Pembroke Dock celebrated its centenary in July 1914, little realising that the country would be at war within a few weeks. A centenary monument was unveiled in Albion Square to mark the occasion.

> This pedestal and lamp were erected by public subscription to commemorate the Centenary of the town of Pembroke Dock and the Royal Dockyard. The town was built almost entirely by the working classes who, by their thrift and industry, erected during the century upwards of 2000 houses. In 1914 the first houses were built on freehold land acquired by the corporation. Population Census 1911 – 11,336. The Royal Dockyard was established in the year 1814. The first ships built were the *Valorous* and *Ariadne*, both being launched on 10 February 1816.

On the other face of the memorial the proclamations of King Edward VII and King George V were noted. Since then the names of three further sovereigns have been added.

This composite postcard, published to commemorate the centenary of the yards and town in 1914, shows, in the centre, the first two vessels launched, the *Ariadne* and *Valorous*.

Following the unveiling of the memorial by the Mayor, Alderman Robinson, on Wednesday 15 July 1914, a complete programme of celebratory events was organised for the people of the town. They loved parades and processions and seized on the chance to celebrate at any time – this was a very special moment in the town's history.

To begin proceedings the Pembroke Dock Military Band, Conductor Mr T. James, played a varied programme of music, commencing with the march 'The Guards'. Their programme included such pieces as 'My Lady Molly', the Welsh National Anthem and 'Immer Fidel'. The concert was followed by a public luncheon at the Royal Edinburgh Hotel, children's teas in the various Sunday Schools of the town, a pageant and a carnival that took hours to wind its way around the streets. A Children's Sports was held and a performance by the Juvenile Pierrots. Then came, for many – the children of the town, certainly – the highlight of the day, a confetti battle that left the streets looking like a war zone. The day finished with a number of Carnival Dances, the main one taking place in the Market Hall.

For the people of Pembroke Dock the centenary celebrations marked the end of one hundred years of glorious achievement. As the memorial declared, the town had been created by their efforts and they were

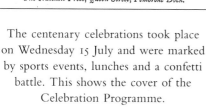

1814—1914

Pembroke Dock Centenary

Programme of Celebrations

WEDNESDAY, JULY 15th, 1914

o

W. ROBINSON, ESQ., MAYOR, CHAIRMAN.

J. GRIEVE, ESQ., EX-MAYOR ⎫ VICE-
G. H. TEESDALE, ESQ., J.P. ⎬ CHAIRMEN.
G. MASON, ESQ. ⎭

W. WILLIAMS, ESQ., TREASURER.
P. MORGAN, HON. SECRETARY.

Price - 1d.

The Nutshell Press, Queen Street, Pembroke Dock.

The centenary celebrations took place
on Wednesday 15 July and were marked
by sports events, lunches and a confetti
battle. This shows the cover of the
Celebration Programme.

Another view of the centenary memorial.

justifiably proud of their achievement. Now it was time to look to the
future. And at that stage the future seemed assured. Nothing could damage
the town or the position that Britain held in the world. If only they had
known what lay ahead!

CHAPTER ELEVEN

Decline and Closure

Groups of soldiers are often to be seen on Edwardian and Victorian postcards. This view shows a group of Royal Garrison Artillery NCOs, complete with mascot, at Pembroke Dock, Christmas 1913.

LESS THAN A MONTH after Pembroke Dock celebrated its centenary the world went to war. As far as the town was concerned it meant a sudden influx of soldiers with the whole of South Pembrokeshire being turned into what was virtually an armed camp.

Within a matter of weeks hundreds of soldiers were crammed into places such as the Defensible and Llanion Barracks, while others were quartered under canvas in the fields alongside. In all, before August was out there were over 4,000 troops mustered in the town prior to shipping out to march, parade and fight on the sands of Palestine or the green

fields of France. The dockyard hurriedly completed its refitting work on the destroyer *Garry*, the ship leaving so hurriedly that the workmen did not even have time to paint her funnels. By mid-August Carr Jetty was protected with a torpedo net and the town, dockyard and various barracks were on a clear war footing.

On the evening of 15 August over 500 people crammed into the Market Hall for the town's first recruiting meeting. The Band of the Welsh Regiment played a selection of martial airs and patriotic tunes and then the audience was regaled with a wide variety of speakers. One of them was Sergeant Fuller, holder of the Victoria Cross, who claimed that he had been in the town for a number of weeks, trying to get men to enlist. The response was always the same – 'I'm working in the dockyard'. He went on to label fit and healthy young men who would make good soldiers but had gone, instead, to work in the dockyard, as cowards and shirkers! Another speaker was Lieutenant R.J. Griffiths of the Welsh Regiment, a Pembrokeshire man himself. According to Vernon Scott in *When the Poppies Bloom Again*, he was equally as scathing about the young men of the town:

> He was walking about at the back of the hall and came across four young men of military age. He asked if they were going to enlist and was told 'No fear! We are earning £3 10 shillings a week in the dockyard and are not fools enough to chuck that up for seven shillings' ... If the men he had spoken to were typical of the kind Pembrokeshire had bred ... he was ashamed – bitterly ashamed. They were not fit to be called men and the army did not want such people. Conscription was the only thing to cure them and officers and senior non-commissioned officers would make their lives hell.

If the speakers thought such attacks would sway the young men of the town they were very much mistaken. At the end of the meeting only ten volunteers came forward and not one of them was from Pembroke Dock. When conscription was introduced two years later, most of the men in Pembroke Dockyard were regarded as carrying out work of national importance and were therefore excluded from military service.

That did not mean that no men from the town joined the army in these years. Charles Breckenbridge was just one of many Welsh soldiers killed when the 38th (Welsh Division) attacked Mametz Wood during the Battle of the Somme in 1916 while Private Thomas George Adams, born in Military Road, Pennar, died of wounds received near Ypres a year later.

A regiment of young volunteers ready to embark on a train at the town station. By the end of the war in 1918 many of the young men in this photograph would be buried in the fields of France and Belgium.

Corporal Mitchell from the town joined the ranks of the fallen the same year. Dozens of men joined the army and survived. When the war ended the town held two Welcome Home events and at one of them conferred the Freedom of the Borough on six Pembroke Dock men who had been decorated during the conflict. The medals won by men like Major Harold Wynne Collins, Bombardier David Leighton and Sergeant James Farthing included the Military Cross, the Military Medal and the Distinguished Service Medal.

Servicemen, whether Pembroke Dock residents or just soldiers who had been posted to the town, were collectively remembered in the Memorial Park, opened in May 1925. Amazingly, the town had not had a park until this time. As in many other British towns, a tank was placed on a plinth in the park, but this was taken away in the early days of the Second World War, presumably for scrap.

Dockyard employees often came in for heavy criticism at this time, one letter writer in the *Pembroke County Guardian* during 1916 describing the place as 'a Government funk hole'. It was undoubtedly an unfair comment as the men in the dockyard were carrying out work of national importance. Without them the vital task of repairing and building ships for the navy would simply not have happened. But these were emotional times and for people with sons, brothers and other relatives serving in France, the sight of healthy young men sitting safely at home – as they undoubtedly saw it – was sometimes too much to bear. So perhaps the criticism was understandable, if not always totally accurate.

Sometimes dockyard employees did not exactly help themselves. In March 1918 fourteen labourers absented themselves from work in the yards in order to attend a football match. The men were dismissed and were promptly called up by the army. However, such happenings did not endear the dockyard workers to the public in general, tending only to confirm the opinion that the dockyard was a place for shirkers and cowards.

Like many other towns in the country, Pembroke Dock suffered badly from food shortages as the war progressed. Such was the violence of popular opinion about this that a dockyard labourer called Reginald Thomas was actually fined £3 for

The Pier, Pembroke Dock. Morgan, Pembroke Dock.

The need to keep the dockyard working kept many Pembroke Dock men out of the forces. This view shows workmen at Hobbs Point fitting out berth – notice the huge sheer legs used for lifting heavy machinery into the newly launched ships.

throwing his dinner onto the kitchen fire in a show of temper. It was considered, in the opinion of the Police Superintendent who brought the charge:

> a dastardly thing ... to have destroyed the food which his wife had obtained and prepared for him.

Strange times indeed! Venereal disease was also widespread in the town during the war years, the huge influx of soldiers, many of whom had picked up the disease while on active service in France, being largely responsible for the epidemic. The town also suffered from a large number of TB cases during this time.

In June 1918 there was tremendous excitement in the town when one of the early tanks was brought into Albion Square as part of 'Tank Week'. The idea was for people to donate money to pay for the cost of a new 'metal monster'. Every night for a week there was entertainment around the tank, the town band playing on a regular basis.

News of the Armistice in November 1918 was received with a huge outpouring of emotion. Ships in the Haven sounded their fog horns and sirens and the guns of the Defensible Barracks were fired in celebration. Soon a military band was marching around the streets of the town and a procession had formed up behind it. The dockyard closed down for the day and every house quickly found a Union Jack to hang out of the window. It was over, the war to end all wars. Now normality could return.

Normality, however, was the very last thing that the town was about to endure. When the guns ceased firing and killing finally stopped, Pembroke Dockyard's future had been firmly and irrevocably sealed. By 1919 it was not a question of whether or not the yards would close, it was more a matter of when!

In actual fact the writing had been on the wall for the dockyard as early as October 1904 when Admiral Sir John Fisher – Jacky as he was universally known – became First Sea Lord. A man of boundless energy and with a clear vision for the future, Fisher was determined to modernise

A war savings rally held in Albion Square in 1917, complete with band and a new invention that was guaranteed to create interest in the town – a tank.

the navy and promptly set about introducing a series of reforms that were to have a profound effect on both the town and dockyard of Pembroke Dock.

Fisher was the man behind the creation of HMS *Dreadnought* in 1906. She was the navy's first turbine driven battleship and was armed with ten 12 inch guns instead of the usual four. Like the *Warrior*, forty years before, her revolutionary design made every other warship in the world obsolete overnight. But, above all, it was Fisher's insistence that the gunboats of Victorian Britain were 'too weak to fight, too slow to run away' that really spelled trouble for Pembroke Dockyard. As far as Fisher was concerned, all gunboats could be scrapped immediately. As this was exactly the type of vessel that Pembroke Dockyard had been specialising in since 1860 it did not take the greatest imagination in the world to realise that the future for the dockyard looked decidedly bleak.

Fisher wanted his new battleships armed with the largest and heaviest calibre guns possible. Accordingly, the *Dreadnought's* 12 inch guns soon grew into the huge 15 inch weapons of the 'Queen Elizabeth' class. As the great 'Navy Race' began, with all other maritime nations hurriedly building giant Dreadnoughts to match the British, it was clear that Pembroke Dock was simply not big enough to cope with ships of this size and complexity. The gunboats might have gone but Pembroke Dockyard had nothing to replace them with.

Fisher also now changed strategic planning for the navy. Germany, he argued, had become Britain's greatest challenge and threat. With the Kaiser demanding parity in sea power and the High Seas Fleet being rapidly created in Kiel, the North Sea was the most likely combat area, should war ever come, and, as far as Jacky Fisher was concerned, that entailed developing a series of naval bases that actually faced the enemy, places such as Harwich, Dover and Scapa Flow. Milford Haven and the relatively tiny dockyard at its eastern end were, really, quite irrelevant.

The rôle of Royal Naval Dockyards was also changing at about this time. With more and more commercial yards now able to build warships – and build them quite efficiently and quite cheaply – there was far more call for the Royal Dockyards to become involved with repair and refitting work. Pembroke Dockyard had never been a great fitting-out yard and to convert it to this purpose now would have involved the huge expense of building dry docks, fitting basins and numerous deep water jetties – all the facilities, in fact, that the place did not possess.

In light of this, in the years leading up to the Great War, Pembroke

HMS *Drake*, probably the most photographed ship in the navy – because of her name – was launched in March 1901. An excess of £22,000 was incurred in her construction.

Dockyard turned its attention to the building of armoured cruisers. Vessels such as the *Essex*, *Cornwall* and *Defence* were powerful and well-armoured ships designed to patrol the distant sea lanes, keeping open the country's vital communication network with its Empire. The *Drake*, an armoured cruiser launched in March 1901 was, for a while, the most photographed ship in the Royal Navy, presumably because of her famous name. An excess of £22,000 was incurred in her construction, the cost of labour exceeding the original estimate by £30,987. Only a saving of £9,000 on materials kept the cost down. *The Times*, with more than a degree of astuteness, commented:

> A good deal of the excess is accounted for by the lack of facilities for completing large ships at the dockyard.

Partly as a result of this criticism, work on finishing Carr Jetty as a deep-water fitting-out berth was hurried to completion. Despite an expenditure of over £100,000 it was a false dawn for the dockyard.

The yards were dealt another crippling blow in the years after 1907 when the battlecruiser concept was developed. The battlecruisers were huge, fast ships that were equipped with heavy guns but, in order to help maintain their speed, were only lightly armoured. It was a mistaken strategy, particularly if they were to be included in the battle line against full-blown battleships, as the serious losses to Beatty's battlecruiser squadron at Jutland

The fast cruiser *Boadicea*, launched in 1908.

– not to mention the loss of the *Hood* during the Second World War – were soon to show. As far as Pembroke Dockyard was concerned, once again the yards were too small to cope with vessels of this size and length.

There was, perhaps, almost a degree of desperation in the way that the yards were now turned to building light scout cruisers. In the main they were beautiful, sleek little ships such as the *Boadicea*, *Blanche* and *Blonde*, but there were only so many light cruisers that the navy needed. Had there been no other problems, no other issues involved, things might have been different. As it was, Jacky Fisher's reforms spelt the end of the road for Pembroke Dockyard.

By 1907, with the yards under-used and under-funded, 700 men were laid off. It was the first time in nearly a hundred years that such a thing had happened. The yards continued to turn out ships of stunning grace and beauty, but some of them did suffer from the serious design flaws that seemed to haunt many Royal Naval ships of the period. The *Duke of Edinburgh*, for example, launched in 1904 and completed two years later, had her 6 inch battery mounted far too low. Consequently, the guns were unworkable in anything like a heavy sea. Her anti-torpedo boat armament was also far from adequate. These faults were remedied when the *Warrior* was built a year later. She was fitted with 7.5 inch guns on the upper deck with fire control platforms in her masts to direct the fire of the guns. Unlike the *Duke of Edinburgh* she was renowned as an excellent sea-boat.

In the years up to 1914 the yards continued to turn out one or, at most, two ships a year. It was, in the words of Commander J. S. Guard:

> a very modest output at a time of hectic naval expansion. One may wonder why the yard was not switched to building destroyers, which were being produced in fairly large numbers at this time … [however] there were commercial yards specialising in such craft who could build them very economically in batches.

During the war years three light cruisers were built and five submarines. With Milford Haven at last becoming well-used as a base for anti-submarine forces patrolling the Western Approaches there was now, by a strange and ironic quirk of fate, a considerable amount of repair and refit work going on in the yards. As a result the workforce increased enormously. By the beginning of 1918 there were over 4,000 men and, for the first time in the yard's history, women also employed. It was the largest number of people ever to work in the dockyard. When future US President Franklin Delano Roosevelt visited the yards in the summer of 1918, in his capacity of Assistant Secretary of the US Navy, he commented that:

The programme for the official Welcome Home held for Pembroke Dock soldiers in June 1920.

Market Hall,

Finis Coronat Opus 1914-1919.

PEMBROKE DOCK

Final Welcome Home

and Presentation of Souvenirs

To its Gallant Boys,

TUESDAY, JUNE 8th, 1920.

Chairman, W. SMITH. Esq., J.P., C.C.
Hon. Secretary, H. M. MILBURN.

THOMAS PRINTER.

Friends of the Men will be admitted to the Hall by the North Door at 7—7.30 p.m.

PROGRAMME
FOR THE
FINAL SECTION OF
OUR BOYS WELCOMED
HOME.

Preparatory to serving High Tea

6.15 p.m., Grace

will be offered by the Rev. Jestyn Jenkins (St. Andrew's)

High Tea.

Selections by the Band.

7 p.m., Thanksgiving

by the Rev. D. T. Davies, (Gilgal)

Interval 7 to 7.30 p.m.

AT

**7.30 p.m.
Smoking Concert
and the Presentation
of Diplomas of Honour,**

Presided over by His Worship the Mayor (O. Davies, Esq.)

Overture by . .
THE TEMPERANCE BAND
under the conductorship of Mr. F. Rees.
Toast—The King—His Worship the Mayor. (Musical Honours).
Chorus—"Comrades in Arms" (by special request)
Pater Male Voice Choir
(Conductor—Mr. John Thomas)
Toast—Our Guests—Coun. W. Smith
Part Song—"Excelsior"
P.M.V. Choir

First Presentation of Diplomas of Honour

Part Song—"Peace to the Souls of the Heroes"—P.M.V. Choir
Response to Toast 2.
Mr. W. Martin (Navy)
Mr. W. H. Morris (Army)
Song—"The Floral Dance"—
Mr. J. Collins

2nd Presentation of Diplomas,

Solo & Chorus—"Killarney"
Mr. G. Russan & Choir
Chorus—"Crossing the Plain"—
P.M.V. Choir

3rd Presentation of Diplomas,

Chorus—"The Crusaders"
P.M.V. Choir
Selection by the Band.
National Anthem

Accompanist—Mr. Frank James.

I was particularly interested to see over 500 women employed in various capacities, some of them even acting as moulders' helpers in the foundry, and all of them doing excellent work.

It was too good to last, and in the months following the end of the war the workforce was reduced by over half. By the end of 1919 the threat of closure was very real.

During 1919 a submarine, the *H52*, was completed and the cruiser *Capetown* was partially built in the yards. She had been laid down at Cammell Lairds and brought round to Pembroke Dock in an effort to keep the workforce busy. Really, however, this was only fitting-out work. The Royal Fleet Auxiliary tanker *Oleander* was launched on 3 May 1922 and to her must go the honour of being the last vessel ever built at Pembroke Dockyard. Even then, her boilers and much of her machinery had been made at other dockyards like Chatham and Devonport in a desperate attempt to spread the workload and keep dockyard maties employed.

A serious fire in the mould loft on 24 July 1922 caused considerable damage, destroying numerous archive records and a priceless collection of old ship models and figure heads. The fire simply served to hasten the inevitable decline.

The RFA tanker *Oleander* was the last ship to be launched from the Royal Naval Dockyard at Pembroke Dock on 26 April 1922. She was sunk by German bombers during the Norwegian campaign in 1940.

The fire at Pembroke Dockyard June 24th 1922. photographed by J.H.Roberts. DrugStores, Neyland, from a distance of over one mile.

On 24 June 1922 a serious fire in the mould loft of the dockyard caused major damage and destroyed a priceless collection of ships figureheads. The fire hastened the decline of the dockyard.

The announcement that Pembroke Dockyard was to close came on Wednesday 2 September 1925. It was a catastrophe for the town and, despite all the anxiety and fears that had been around for months, came as a thunderbolt to the population. Nobody had wanted to believe that it would really come to this. The community had been created to build ships. Now its reason for existence had been snatched away.

Many people have written about the closure but, in an article on the last days of the dockyard in the *West Wales Guardian*, dated 20 February 1976, Llewellyn Thomas probably came closest to capturing the mood of the time:

> Despite all the forebodings few Pembrokians cared even to contemplate the closure of the yard. Among them ... was the sitting MP for the County, Sir Charles Price. Only a month or so before the Admiralty made the closure announcement he severely criticised a London newspaper's assertion that the days of Pembroke as a Royal Dockyard were numbered. Opening the annual St Patrick's fête at Pennar he cheered the whole neighbourhood when he claimed that not only was the yard not to be closed but that there were plans afoot to enlarge it towards the west.

Pembroke Dock cannot be separated from the sea. Old wrecks and discarded vessels have always been a common sight. This photograph is of an old trawler that lay for many years on the shingle and mud beach at the bottom of Gordon Street

Quite what world Sir Charles was living in was not clear but he must have given some faint hope to desperately worried dockyard workers. There had never been plans to extend the dockyard. The Secretary of the Admiralty was clear that there had been, and would continue to be, a diminution in the amount of construction and repair work needing to be carried out in the Royal Dockyards. In his statement announcing the closure he said:

> this renders it inevitable that there shall be a considerable reduction in dockyard numbers. The Board have decided that in this new situation the best method of securing efficiency and economy will be to reduce the number of establishments. The dockyards at Rosyth and Pembroke will therefore be reduced to a care and maintenance basis.

What that meant was that the yards would be 'mothballed', the plant and machinery regularly overhauled and maintained in case there should ever be a need to open them up again. But as a building yard, the place would be shut! Over 1,000 men were to be discharged by the end of the month while the remaining workforce would be gradually reduced over the following year. Established men in the dockyard would be offered the option of taking their pensions or of re-deploying to other dockyards. But for casual or hired workers there was only the dole queue.

From right across the town and county there were immediate protests. The Mayor of Pembroke Borough, Alderman W.W. George, and his successor, Councillor George Brown, were strident in their defence of the yards and deputations were hastily despatched to London and elsewhere. A petition was sent to Prime Minister Stanley Baldwin, stressing the complete lack of alternative employment. And, said the petition, it was not just the dockyard employees who would suffer. With the dockyard closed, all tradesmen in the town would be ruined. Families would fall apart. Social and economic ruin loomed for everyone. Supporters estimated that upwards of 16,000 men and women in the county of Pembrokeshire were dependent on the dockyard for their livelihood. All of them would lose out when the yard closed its doors!

Gwilym Lloyd George, soon to be returned to Parliament at the expense of the ill-informed Charles Price, admitted to being amazed at the decision – Chatham, he declared, was far more vulnerable to air attack than Pembroke Dock would ever be. In the light of future events, his statement was possibly as mistaken and badly judged as his predecessor's comments about the future of the yards.

In the end, it was all of no use, the Admiralty had made its decision. The yards would close. This they duly did, on 31 May 1926. By September of that year there were 1,400 men on the dole in the town while, as Lawrence Phillips has said, by 1927:

Pembroke Dock is now 'almost entirely a town of unemployed and pensioners' ... The direct consequence of State policy was thus to destroy a town; between 1921 and 1931 some 3,500 people, a quarter of the town's inhabitants, migrated, while in 1937 over half of the insured population of the borough were unemployed.

Old men and old memories, all that remained of the Royal Naval Dockyard after its closure in 1926.

As many had predicted, the consequences of the dockyard's closure were widespread and varied. Many of the skilled dockyard workmen had no option but to leave the area. Some of the established men went into jobs in other Royal Dockyards; some even sailed off to new lives in the dockyards of places such as Bermuda and Malta. But these were the lucky ones. For most ex-dockyard men there was only the dole queue and the memories of what had once been taken very much for granted.

Businesses all over Pembrokeshire went into liquidation, but in Pembroke and Pembroke Dock the tradesmen were particularly badly hit. Sybil Edwards, in *The Story of the Milford Haven Waterway*, has recorded the case of just one Pembroke tradesman who felt the effects of the closure:

> The baker and grocer Hugh Edward Hall of Main Street, Pembroke, blamed bad trade caused by the closure of the dockyard, heavy bank charges and the high running cost of his motor vehicles for his £4,000 bankruptcy.

Only three areas in the whole of Wales had a higher percentage of unemployment. And this was at a time of unprecedented deprivation, when the future King Edward VIII had visited Merthyr and declared 'Something must be done!' What might he have said if he had visited Pembroke Dock instead?

Some degree of respite was offered to the people of the town in 1931 when the Royal Air Force made a vitally important decision to establish a flying boat base inside the old dockyard walls. There had been talk of

After the closure of the dockyard in 1926 depression loomed. It was only partially alleviated by the arrival of the RAF four years later when a flying boat base was established in the eastern part of the yards.

Various aircraft served at PD, as the base was universally known. This photograph shows a Royal Navy Fairy IIIF float plane, probably attached to the 2nd Cruiser Squadron, in the Haven, circa 1930.

With the coming of the RAF came new technology. This shows a giant aircraft hanger, designed to house the famous Sunderland flying boats, in the process of being built.

View from Barrack Hill, Pembroke Dock.

an air base in the area for some time and sea planes had already landed, a number of times, on the Haven. It was useful practice or maybe even advanced reconnaissance!

The water just off the dockyard was relatively deep and sheltered. The river or estuary was quite calm, at least at most times of the year, and was also wide open. There were no obstacles such as overhanging hills or islands and rocks. In fact, the very qualities that had brought the Admiralty to the area in the first place were also ideal for the flying boats and sea planes of the 1930s and 1940s.

The flying boat most commonly associated with Pembroke Dock is the giant but graceful Sunderland. This view shows one of the aircraft belonging to 201 Squadron.

For several years a unique sight on the Haven was the ugly and ungainly floating dock, used for maintenance of flying boats while they were still on the water. This rare shot shows the dock with a seaplane on board while another comes in to land close by.

The sea planes were meant to stay at Pembroke Dock for only a few short months. As it turned out, the RAF remained in occupation for 29 years. The first aircraft based at PD, as the base quickly became known throughout the service, belonged to 210 Squadron, their Supermarine Southamptons flying to the Haven from Felixstowe in June 1931. New barrack blocks were soon built within the old walls as well as a wide slipway. This was necessary in order to beach the flying boats for maintenance and repair. Two huge aircraft hangers were also built, enormous structures which then, and now, dominated the town as surely as the old covered building slips of the dockyard in the nineteenth century.

Wing Commander Bob Leckie was the first station commander but, undoubtedly, the most famous of all PD's officers was Arthur Harris. He was later to be immortalised as 'Bomber' Harris, the man who masterminded and oversaw the bombing offensive against Germany during the Second World War.

The 1930s saw a gradual and inevitable build-up towards war as Hitler and his legions began to mass and march across Germany and much of Eastern Europe. In consequence there was a rapid build-up of RAF personnel in PD during this time. The original Southampton flying boats were superseded by Stranraers and Singapores and then, in the immediate pre-war years, came the arrival of the famous Sunderlands, the aircraft with which the air base at Pembroke Dock will always be associated. The very first Sunderland in the town appeared at the station's Empire Air Day in the summer of 1938. This was only a fleeting visit, however, but the giant aircraft soon returned – this time in ever greater numbers.

In the years ahead, the giant flying boats became a familiar sight. But to begin with there was only amazement. How could such gigantic machines ever get into the air, people asked? The Sunderlands weren't the only strange sight for the people of Pembroke Dock. Early in 1932 the strange and ungainly shape of a floating dock was moored in the Haven. Known locally as HMS *Flat Iron*, the dock weighed somewhere in the region of 1,000 tons and was designed by John Narberth who had begun his working life as a shipwright in the dockyard before rising to become Assistant Director of Naval Construction at the Admiralty.

The floating dock was ugly but practical. The after-deck could be partially submerged to allow two small flying boats to be loaded and then raised to bring the aircraft clear of the water. However, as flying boats became larger and shore-based repair techniques improved, HMS *Flat Iron* gradually became obsolete and she finally disappeared from the Haven around the time of the Munich Crisis in 1938.

As the world galloped rapidly towards war once more, the people of Pembroke Dock knew that their town would have an important role to play. The Sunderlands, the mothballed dockyard and the military forces would all be vital factors in the desperate and dramatic days ahead.

CHAPTER TWELVE

War Again – and Up to Date

P EMBROKE DOCK SUFFERED BADLY at the hands of the Luftwaffe
  during the Second World War. The moment that war was declared on
3 September 1939 the old dockyard was opened up once more. This time
it did not build ships but was used as a repair and refit yard. The air base
with its mighty Sunderlands was, of course, a major target. On occasions
almost a hundred aircraft could be seen on the waters of the Haven. The
Germans would have been foolish not to see the enormity of the target.

   The first raid came in early July 1940, bombs falling harmlessly into the
Haven between Pembroke Dock and Neyland and causing damage only
to the river's fish stocks. It was followed by several other small raids but

The Admiralty oil tanks at Pennar were bombed in August 1940, creating what was, at the time, the largest fire in Britain since the Great Fire of London in 1666. The fire raged for eighteen days. In this view a huge cloud of smoke hangs above the town.

The Pembroke Dock fire brigade is shown here just after the end of the war. Ted Owens, the youngest firemen present during the fight to quell the flames, stands in the centre of the back row.

they were only minor skirmishes when compared to the enormity of what was to follow.

On Monday 19 August 1940 three German Junkers 88 bombers, escorted by two ME 109 fighters, flew in over the Pembrokeshire coast and deposited their bombs on to the oil tanks at Pennar, high up on the ridge overlooking the town and dockyard. These tanks were strategically important to the Royal Navy. They contained thousands of gallons of essential fuel oil for the ships that were waging the Battle of the Atlantic, keeping the sea lanes open. The Germans had attempted to bomb them before but this time one of the bombs hit its mark. A terrific explosion echoed around the town, rocking the houses in nearby Llanreath and Pennar and making everyone start with fear. It was followed by a huge column of smoke that leapt into the air and hung there like a Sword of Damocles for the next eighteen days.

Ted Owens was then a youngster in the town, acting as unpaid voluntary messenger boy for the local fire brigade:

I was in our garden when the tanks were bombed. I shouted to my mam, 'Look at that plane.' You could see the bombs dropping – no sound but you could see them. Of course, once they got up momentum you could hear them. When the bang came I ran through the house to the front door because that was the direction it came from. I could

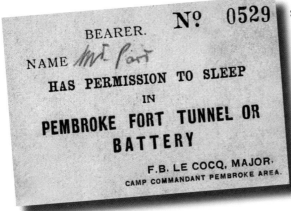

BEARER. Nº 0529

NAME Mr Part

HAS PERMISSION TO SLEEP
IN
PEMBROKE FORT TUNNEL OR
BATTERY

F.B. LE COCQ, MAJOR.
CAMP COMMANDANT PEMBROKE AREA.

see this big pall of smoke going up. I didn't realise then that this column of smoke was the fire. I thought it was just the dust and debris.

At the precise moment the bomb fell, two Pennar farmers, Fred and Ronnie Phillips, were working in the field alongside the tanks. The two brothers came from a well-known local family, one of their relatives already having been elected town Mayor. As far as Fred was concerned, the attack turned him into something of a celebrity. The blast of the bomb lifted him off his feet and deposited him twenty yards away, at the foot of a hayrick, stunned, bruised and winded. He was the town's first civilian casualty of the war. Ronnie, buffeted and half blinded by the force of the explosion, fought to control the horses that made up the threshing team. It was a hopeless task. The terrified animals fled. It was another two weeks before Ronnie's son Jim was able to recover the last of the horses.

Just one oil tank had been hit but already it was a mass of engulfing flames. News of the raid and of the damage to the oil tank was quickly passed to the Pembroke Dock Fire Brigade and immediately Fire Chief Arthur Morris and his team of part-time firemen leapt into action. Arthur Morris was the brother-in-law of Fred and Ronnie Phillips, having married their sister Lizzie, and as he sped up Military Road towards the blazing tank, past his house, he had little idea that he would not be going to bed again for the next two weeks.

Despite the heroic efforts of the firemen the fire spread steadily from one tank to the next. Hurried appeals were sent to brigades from all over the country, asking for firemen and fire appliances to rush to Pembroke Dock and help in the fight. They came in their hundreds but, at that early stage, nobody had any real idea of what was facing them. John Walsh and Hubert 'Buzzer' Reynolds were two of the Cardiff contingent:

I think we'd got as far as St Clears when we noticed the cloud. We didn't realise what was going on until we got a bit further and by then, of course, we were right in the middle of it. (Hubert 'Buzzer' Reynolds)

The Second World War brought immediate problems for Pembroke Dock, one of which was the threat of air raids. This ticket gave permission for the bearer to sleep in the tunnel that led from the Defensible Barracks rather than risk being bombed.

One of our boys said, 'Hey, look at that.' When we looked out there was a great big pall of smoke in the air, going over. We said 'That's not the fire we're going to, is it?' Of course it was. The whole tank farm was on fire. (John Walsh)

Eventually, twenty-two fire brigades were involved, over 600 men, the Pembroke Dock oil tank fire becoming the largest conflagration that Britain had seen since the Great Fire of London in 1666. The fire raged for eighteen days and at times the firemen felt as if they were fighting a losing battle, as John Walsh remembered:

It was a sight I'll never forget. Oh, the flames, they were thirty or forty feet up in the sky and you wouldn't believe the width of them. You take an oil tank – well, there were flames that size going up into the air. And then the smoke. And oil dropping down. It was really frightening. You couldn't go too close because it was so hot. What we were doing was cooling the unaffected tanks and the ones on fire. But as one tank seemed to empty another would catch fire. That's how it went.

In the end eleven of the eighteen tanks were destroyed, their valuable oil lost, burned and spread into the ether or running in a molten

The funeral cortège of the five Cardiff firemen killed while fighting the blaze makes its way down the street from the town mortuary.

At the end of the fire eleven oil tanks were destroyed and 38,000,000 gallons of valuable oil had been lost. This photograph shows the last of the tanks shortly before demolition – the clubhouse of the South Pembs Golf Club now stands on the site.

Arthur Morris, fire chief during the war (right), is shown here with members of his family. Never a 'Yes man,' Arthur Morris was overlooked in the distribution of medals and awards so liberally given out after the crisis.

river down Military Road. Scores of firemen were injured and burned. Tragically, on 22 August, five firemen from the Cardiff Brigade were killed when the wall of a burning tank split open and the oil engulfed them. The men are still remembered every year when a ceremony is held on the site, now the car park of the South Pembs Golf Club. Their names are recorded – Frederick George Davies, Clifford Miles, Ivor John Kilby, Trevor Charles Morgan and John Frederick Thomas – and their sacrifice was not in vain, as by their efforts, they undoubtedly helped to save the town of Pembroke Dock.

In the wake of the disaster controversy reigned. Arthur Morris, hero of the hour, was passed over in the awards that were liberally given to so many others. Morris was never a 'yes man' and was always regarded as a fireman's fireman – had he been critical of some aspect of the operation? No-one ever knew. The town of Pembroke Dock was stunned but, despite protestations, nothing was ever done and Arthur Morris went to his grave, many years later, tight-lipped and modest, making little comment on the affair.

There were many other air raids during the war years as the Luftwaffe, working on faulty intelligence information, was convinced that the dockyard was a ship building yard. The town had its first fatalities a short while after the oil tank fire when an elderly couple were killed by a direct hit on their house and grocery business in Bush Street.

Then came the raid that everyone had been expecting and dreading. As Bill Richards has written:

There was an inescapable feeling that one night it would be Pembroke Dock's turn and, sure enough, it came on May 12th (1941), when

The house of Dr Stewart on the corner of Lower Gwyther Street and Apley Terrace, badly damaged in a raid on the night of 11–12 May 1941.

the town was almost reduced to a shambles under the terrific bombardment.

That night a large force of enemy bombers attacked the dockyard and air base, dropping dozens of bombs in a saturation raid that lasted for over half an hour. Land mines, high explosives and incendiary bombs rained down on the streets and houses. The dockyard and RAF station were, largely, missed in the attack although an ordnance factory in the town and the gas works were hit. Nearly 2,000 houses were damaged, the Pier Hotel, the Three Crowns and the Prince Albert pub being destroyed by direct hits. Thirty-two people were killed, thirty civilians and two servicemen, while dozens more were injured by flying glass and shrapnel. Ferry boat sailings the following day between Hobbs Point and Neyland had to be cancelled due to the danger of mines in the Haven.

The death toll and damage to the town for this one raid alone was immense. When you consider the size and population of Pembroke Dock they were probably as high, proportionally, as those endured in almost any town in Britain during the war years. After the raid the town was, virtually, abandoned most nights as people fled to quieter parts of the area during the danger hours. The military assisted, sending trucks around the streets to pick up and transport many of those who wished to leave the town. Others simply walked or rode their bicycles towards Pembroke, Freshwater East and places where the threat of bombing did not loom so large. The long lines of men, women and children struggling down

Heavy bombing caused serious damage to the town during the war. This shows bombed out houses in Gwyther Street

More bomb damage
in the town.

Bush Hill have been compared to the famous images of French or Polish refugees fleeing from the advancing Germans in the early days of the war. Such descriptions are undoubtedly accurate.

Griffith John Jones was in the RAF at Pembroke Dock during some of the raids and his memories remain vivid:

> We came off duty this one night, about midnight, I think, and went out through the old dockyard gates. Then it was uphill to the school where we were billeted – I think it was the old National School that later became the Employment Office for the town. I was in bed, asleep. I never heard any alarm or siren. The first thing I knew was this loud whistling, a bomb dropping close by. I was up and under the bed in double quick time. Then there was a terrific crash as the whole stick of bombs exploded. Lots of houses were demolished. They made a terrible mess of the town.

The last big German raid on Pembroke Dock occurred on the night of 11 June 1941. Due to the nightly exodus, the town was largely unpopulated at the time but the attack was heavy and prolonged. Thousands of incendiary bombs were dropped, fires springing up wherever they fell. Two teenage ARP messengers, the youngest one, Arthur Kavanagh, being just thirteen years old, were killed when a stick of bombs fell right alongside them as they attempted to put out one of the incendiaries. Two other residents were also killed, a man helping his wife to escape into the fields and a serving RAF man who also died while trying to save his wife.

Ted Owens, the young messenger boy with the local fire brigade, has clear memories of the raid. Although he went on to fight with distinction in the Royal Marine Commandos, this attack on Pembroke Dock was almost his last night on earth:

> I was standing in the doorway of the fire station. The engine was still inside. I said 'Oh, look, there's a parachute coming down.' I never thought it could be a land mine. The next thing it went off. The explosion blew me backwards, right to the back end of the fire engine. There were shelves there, all with tins of paint on. The whole lot came down on top of me – luckily none of them opened. I was knocked out. They carried me in and put me onto one of the fold-up beds. The next thing I can remember is somebody washing my mouth with a sponge, trying to get rid of all the dust.

The Sunderlands of PD were heavily engaged in convoy duties during the war, making long-range sorties out over the Atlantic, searching for enemy U-boats. The best-known episode in PD's aerial war came in 1943 when a Sunderland from the base was attacked by eight JU 88s over the Bay of Biscay. Bristling with guns, the Sunderland was no easy target and three enemy planes were shot down, a fourth being severely damaged. Despite having several crew members injured and one killed, the Sunderland managed to limp back home. An aircraft from PD made history when, in May 1943, she landed on the grass runway of nearby Angle aerodrome after being holed during a rescue at sea. It was the first time a flying boat had successfully touched down on land.

Griffith John Jones was posted to PD at the end of 1940. He was later to log up a flying time of over 1,400 hours, taking part in several attacks on U-boats and then, because Coastal Command was needed to make up the numbers, in the first 1,000 bomber raid on Bremen. At Pembroke Dock, however, he was not fully operational and spent most of his time in Signals. He recalls an incident in the Haven at this time:

> We were up on the Barrack Hill this day, just sitting there in the sunlight. It was a beautiful day and as we were off duty we were taking advantage of the weather. We watched this old Walrus flying boat make its approach to land on the Haven. Everything was so calm but then the Walrus must have hit a log or something because as she came in to land she went up and turned three somersaults in the air. We sat there and watched it and we thought, 'Well, that's it, the crew are dead.' But you know something? They all walked away, unharmed.

In addition to the RAF, Canadian and Australian flyers were also based in the town and in 1943 an American squadron arrived. For several months their Catalinas, or PBYs as they were more properly called, kept company with the Sunderlands on the waters of Milford Haven.

The last ship to be built in the Royal Naval Dockyard, the RFA tanker *Oleander*, was lost during the war, being sunk by German bombers during the Norway campaign of 1940. It was the end of an era.

When peace finally came in the spring of 1945 it was time for the people of Pembroke Dock to take stock. The damage to property had been immense and the re-building programme took several years to reach its conclusion. Helped by the War Damage Commission, the repairs did at least give some employment to the men of the town, many of them newly discharged from the armed forces. By general reckoning, however, it still took two years for all the roofs in the town to be repaired!

Celebrations to mark VE Day. This view shows the bunting and beginning of celebrations in King Street.

An estate of pre-fabricated houses was built at Bufferland and, although designed to last for just ten years, they were still in existence thirty years later. In the 1950s and 1960s, two new council estates were created in separate parts of the town, offering alternative accommodation to people from those houses that were either beyond repair or too old and out of date.

A number of new factories were built and businesses established in the eastern area known as Kingswood during these years. They were designed to produce metal goods and textiles and, for a while, one of Britain's premier producers of roller skates had its headquarters on this early example of an industrial estate.

The town's Temperance Hall had once stood proudly on the corner of Lewis Street and Dimond Street. However, it had been seriously damaged by bombs and was unusable. The place was rebuilt, renamed the Pater Hall and used as the location for countless dances and variety shows ever since. In the years since 1986 it has also served as the headquarters of the newly formed Pembroke Dock Town Council. The twin towns of Pembroke and Pembroke Dock, previously always joined together as Pembroke Borough, finally split in 1986, each going their own separate ways in terms of civic office and local politics.

The crest of Pembroke Borough Urban Authority. This version, for the Sanitary Department, has the flags flying inwards, in opposite directions. Other versions have the flags flying outwards.

In the years after 1945 there were many other changes to which the people of Pembroke Dock had to adjust. In August 1949 the last of the town's 146 gas lamps was taken away while an historic public house, the Globe – arguably the oldest pub in Pembroke Dock – was finally knocked down.

With the passing of a new Education Act the secondary schools in the town were reorganised, the Coronation becoming a Secondary Modern, the old County taking on a new identity as a Grammar School. In 1955 the Grammar School moved to new, purpose-built premises on Bush Hill, midway between the two towns. Purpose-built they may have been but, being situated on the side of a steep hill, there was more than a little subsidence in the building. Several generations of school children passed on the joke that the pieces of glass cemented into the school walls – really there to measure the amount of movement in the building – were all that were actually holding the place together.

When the new school opened Bush House, the previous home of the Meyrick family, also became part of the school. For many years it ran as a boarding house for boys from all over Britain who wished to come to Pembroke to study agriculture at the school farm. It was a unique arrangement but one which, by the late 1970s, was obsolete. In 1973 the Grammar School and the Coronation merged into a new comprehensive and Bush House was eventually closed.

Bush House had been the scene of one of the area's most famous ghost stories. During conversion work on the house in 1954 the night watchman, a Pembroke Dock man called David James, claimed he saw a man approaching him one evening. The man was between 60 and 70 years of age and had three dogs with him. James stated that he spoke to the man in both English and Welsh but received no answer. Indeed, neither the man nor the dogs made any noise at all. The next year workmen in the house are said to have heard banging and knocking inside the house but its source could not be located.

One evening three of the workmen from Manchester, rather than find and pay for accommodation, decided to sleep in the house. Almost at once strange happenings began. Their lamp flickered and the flame grew dim and one of the men, an Italian called Tony, had the coats he was using as a blanket pulled off him by an unknown hand. The next night, on the path outside, they saw a woman in a white or grey crinoline gown. She was surrounded by an eerie light. The three workmen promptly fled and spent the rest of the night in the new school. With hindsight, in the clear light of day, it is easy to see what happened at Bush House. An old, creaking building, some high-spirited workmen playing tricks on their excitable Italian friend – and the origins of another ghost tale can be identified.

Everyone loves a good mystery tale, however, and the story began to spread that, back in 1802, a local squire had shot his wife and covered it

Bush House, the home of the Meyrick family. The Meyricks were the landowners who sold much of the land to the Admiralty in order to build the dockyard – could they be regarded as the 'founding fathers' of the town?

Bush House, Pembroke.

up by saying that she had died from pneumonia. No record of any such death or event exists for any of the houses built on the site – there have been three in all – but the legend of the 'grey lady' was too good to ignore and continued to be in vogue with the boarders until Bush House closed in the late 1970s.

Back in 1955, four local men – journalist Vernon Scott, photographer Stanley Mansel, sportsman Matt Arnold and local solicitor James Meyrick Owen – who was, incidentally, related to the original owners of the house – entered into the spirit of the affair. They volunteered to spend a night in the house to 'uncover the truth'. This they duly did, amidst great public interest and publicity but the intrepid ghost hunters saw no spirits or unearthly spectres. Perhaps they had been frightened off by the cameras!

For a few years after the war Pembroke Dock basked in a degree of prosperity. It was yet another false dawn. As Prime Minister Harold Macmillan said 'You've never had it so good.' A hammer blow hit the town when, in February 1957, it was announced that the RAF station would be closed. The old Sunderlands had become obsolete and there were no plans to replace them with other flying boats. It was a blow to the town and one that was felt by the RAF personnel as well. Bill Williams had been posted to PD only the year before, settling with his family in the new RAF quarters along Stranraer Avenue in Pennar:

> I hadn't really wanted a posting to Pembroke Dock – I didn't even know where the place was – but when I got there I was enchanted with it all. The town, the people, the scenery on the coast, it was all wonderful. I remember going up to Military Road of an evening, to a pub called the Kilwendege. The blokes in there made you so welcome. I remember them all singing a song about the Mochyn Ddu, the whole pub used to join in. It was a great time but I was only there about a year and then the RAF decided to close the station down. I was really upset about that.

For almost thirty years the flying boats had been a common sight along the Haven. Generations of Pembroke Dock children had grown up with the deep-throated roar of the Sunderland's Pegasus engines vibrating in their ears. Now, with the advent of jet aircraft that could traverse the globe in a few brief hours the day of the cumbersome old veterans was finally over. The last of the Sunderlands left the town in March 1959 and the station returned to Admiralty control.

The town had not quite finished with Sunderlands, however. In March

The Pembroke Coast Express ran for several years between London and Pembroke Dock, bringing thousands of tourists to the county. This card shows the range of food available in the restaurant car.

1961, watched by thousands of eager spectators, many of them with more than a few fond tears in their eyes, Sunderland ML 824 landed on the waters of the Haven. Presented to the new Sunderland Trust by its owners, the French Navy, the flying boat was brought ashore and put on show as 'The Last Sunderland'. The weather and salt air took their toll on the old plane, however, and in 1971 it was decided to present the Sunderland to the RAF Museum at Hendon. Sunderland ML 824 duly left the town and is now on view in the museum's Battle of Britain Hall.

By 1959 people in Pembroke Dock could be excused for feeling a little glum and fatalistic. The dockyard had gone, the RAF had disappeared. Now only the army was left. And when the announcement came in 1966 that Llanion Barracks were also to close there was a sad inevitability about it all. Over the years many famous men had been stationed in the town, from Gordon of Khartoum to Arthur Lowe, the actor who later made his name as Captain Mainwaring in *Dads' Army*. Lowe was based in the old Defensible Barracks, and it is interesting to wonder if his interpretation of the pompous Captain owes its origin to watching some of the local Pembroke Dock characters, civilians or military men, in action.

The newly crowned Queen Elizabeth II landed in the town during August 1955, her first ever visit to Pembrokeshire. Sailing up the Haven on the new Royal Yacht *Britannia*, the first Royal Yacht for over 100 years not to have been built at Pembroke Dockyard, the Queen came ashore at the RAF Station Pier for a brief but welcome visit. In the great days of the dockyard huge celebratory arches made of wood and flowers had always been set up over the roads of the town whenever a launch was about to take place. In a move highly reminiscent of these grand days a 'welcome arch' was built at the top of Prospect Place for the visit of the

The last Sunderland. In 1961 Sunderland ML824, a gift from the French Navy, returned to the town and was preserved as a museum piece inside the walls of the base for ten years. She finally left Pembroke Dock in 1971 and is now exhibited at the Battle of Britain Museum.

Queen. It is doubtful that she ever saw it, but the sentiment was what really mattered.

There have been many attempts to breathe life back into the once vibrant area and town of Pembroke Dock. For many years the Royal Navy maintained a small presence in the western part of the dockyard, where a Mooring and Marine Salvage Depot was situated but it was only ever a tiny reflection of what had once been.

In the immediate post-war days the firm of R. S. Hayes opened a small ship repair yard in part of the old yards. In 1955 the firm converted a former German cargo vessel, the *Empire Frome*, into the cable ship *Ocean Layer*. In July the following year the trawler *Norrard Star* was launched from the yard, the last major vessel to be launched at Pembroke Dock. For thirty years the trawler operated out of nearby Milford before being, finally, beached off Front Street in 1992.

The two Pembroke Dock ferry boats, the *Cleddau King* and *Cleddau Queen*, were built for the County Council at the yards of Hancocks Shipbuilding Company in Front Street. The *Queen* was launched in January 1956 as an oil-fired steam paddler and the *King* followed six years later. With ramp access, the *King* was a diesel-powered vessel that lasted until 1975 when the Cleddau Bridge was built and made her obsolete at last. Her final fare-paying trip was made on 8 March 1975.

Rumours began to circulate in the early 1950s that the Milford Haven area might be chosen as a centre for the new oil industry. The giant tankers needed somewhere with plenty of deep water and the Haven seemed to be perfect for their requirements. And in due course the expected refineries arrived. By the end of the 1960s jetties and plants had been built along the waterway for firms such as Esso, BP, Regent (later Texaco), Gulf and Amoco. The directors of the ship repair and building firm of R.S.Hayes realised the possibilities and quickly turned their attention to rope running. This was a necessary element in the docking of any ship and the Hayes firm, Marine and Port Services as it became known, was soon busy carrying the ropes from the giant tankers across to the dolphins on the jetties in tiny but incredibly powerful 'rope runners'. The firm also often supplied the tankers, much of the produce being taken down river in an old Clyde puffer.

The company was bought by the Milford Haven Port Authority in 1977 and a series of developments saw the eventual creation of the Port of Pembroke, a deep water wharf being built in the eastern part of the old yard. It meant a degree of employment in the area but the success of the venture was always limited and closure never far away. The company eventually went into receivership before being taken over by the Port Authority. The wharf has all the facilities and potential for a great deal of cargo handling — when and how this will be exploited remains to be seen.

A much more significant development in the town was the creation of the Ro-Ro ferry terminal in the dockyard in 1979. For several years

The Royal Yacht *Britannia* moored off the town during the visit of Queen Elizabeth II to the county in 1955.

the B & I ferries plied the route between Pembroke Dock and Rosslare in southern Ireland, the first voyage having been made by the *Connaught* in May 1979. The service was suspended for economic reasons in 1986 but two years later Irish Ferries began operating out of the port and recommenced sailings to Eire.

A new road was built into the former dockyard, an entrance being opened in the old wall close to the town market and this is the route that heavy lorries and tourists now take when they arrive in the town. Unless, that is, the ferry service is disrupted like it was for three weeks in December 2005 when a number of the crew members barricaded themselves into the engine room of the *Isle of Innishmorn* as a protest against the introduction of cheap labour from eastern Europe. It was a 'sit-in' that grabbed the national headlines and was mirrored by a similar action in Holyhead.

Reflecting the world-wide situation, these days the oil industry in Milford Haven has been significantly reduced. The refineries are still working and the tankers still sail into the Haven but it is nothing like the vibrant port it once was. Back in the 1960s and 1970s, the various refineries and pumping stations provided much work for the people of the town, either by working in the plants as process operators or helping to build them in the first place. Similarly, the construction of a Power Station for the Central Electricity Generating Board on the shores of the Haven during the 1960s gave even more opportunity for work. Building the Cleddau Bridge was yet another opening for the men of the town.

After the closure of the Royal Naval Dockyard several small shipping companies set up business in the old yards. This shows workmen in the shipyard of R S Hayes in the 1950s.

A ferry terminal was built in the eastern part of the old dockyard in 1979, providing a base to take passengers to Ireland and continuing the town's long involvement with the sea.

The new road into the old yards, ready for the ferry port traffic, is shown here during its construction in the late 1980s and and early 1990s.

End of the line – the single railway track which ran into the dockyard, here partially covered over in the 1980s. It was soon to disappear for ever as modern buildings and developments took over.

The Cleddau Bridge, spanning the waters between Pembroke Dock and the north shore of the Haven, was opened on 23 May 1975, the opening having been delayed by a tragic collapse during construction.

The ferry between Hobbs Point and Neyland had always been the shortest, if not always the most reliable, route across the Haven. If there was a heavy autumn fog hanging across the river then the ferries simply would not run – only if the crew could see the other side would they venture out across the water. Such a situation was not acceptable in the late twentieth century. After much debate it was decided, in the late 1960s, that a box girder bridge should be constructed across the waterway.

Unfortunately, on the afternoon of 3 June 1970 disaster hit the enterprise. The southern section of the bridge suddenly collapsed as a box girder section was being moved into place and four workmen were killed. Several others were injured and it was another five years before the bridge was finally completed and opened for public use.

These days little of the old dockyard is left. The huge building sheds were demolished soon after closure and now even the slipways have largely disappeared, swallowed up, first, by the needs of the flying boats and, lately, by the infrastructure around the ferry terminal. The walls that once surrounded the establishment remain largely intact – they will probably still be there in another hundred years' time. The same can be said of many of the officers' quarters and offices. The Dockyard Chapel, though, has led something of a chequered life, being used as the Garrison Theatre for a few years after the dockyard closed and finishing its career as a Motor Museum. By the early 1990s, however, the place was lying empty, lead stripped from its roof and the insides gutted and damaged by fire. After numerous legal wranglings over the ownership of the chapel, Pembrokeshire County Council issued a compulsory purchase order and took possession in November 2003.

The yards have gone, the town remains – a modern view of the town of Pembroke Dock.

With backing from the Heritage Lottery Fund, work began on the restoration of the chapel in 2004. A totally new roof and new window frames enabled the restoration of decorative plaster cornices and mouldings. The work is now complete and the chapel has been restored to its Victorian splendour. Maybe, just maybe, the wheel is beginning to come full circle.

For over fifty years the hulk of the old iron clad *Warrior*, the same vessel that had almost caused the closure of Pembroke Dockyard when she was launched in 1860, had been moored as a pontoon for the Admiralty below their oil tanks at Llanion. She had been offered for sale in April 1929 but as there were no takers the Admiralty simply had her towed to Pembroke Dock by the tugs *St Clears* and *St Mellons*. She was duly moored there as a floating jetty.

To some extent it was a sad end for a once-great warship. On the other hand it was also quite fortunate as her rôle meant that she had not been scrapped like so many other great vessels that had outlived their usefulness. She may have been forgotten by the Lords of the Admiralty but all the while she was carrying out a more than useful rôle. Quite apart from anything else, countless Pembroke Dock children had fished off her stern or gazed at her from sailing boats on the river and everyone knew that this was once a famous ship. When, in the more enlightened days of the 1970s, the decision to preserve the *Warrior* was made, it was an announcement that was greeted with joy from the people of the town.

The old *Warrior* was finally towed from the Haven on 29 August 1979 and taken to Hartlepool where she was restored to her full Victorian glory. Today she lies alongside Nelson's *Victory* in Portsmouth where she is on public view as one of the most important and significant ships ever to grace the Royal Navy.

To some extent the fate of the old *Warrior* reflects the fate and plight of the town of Pembroke Dock – hanging in, as they say, until a better and, perhaps, more enlightened time comes along. The town has had a great past. Its future is not yet certain. But it looks to that future with hope and enthusiasm. One day the town's boat will come in and that will be something worth waiting for.

Conclusion

THE SENSE OF HISTORY remains strong in Pembroke Dock. That is understandable. In a short period of just 112 years the dockyard built over 260 ships, ranging from sleek cruisers and fast gunboats to elegant Royal Yachts and giant pre-Dreadnought battleships. Its RAF station was the largest flying boat base in the world, the Sunderlands playing a crucial role in defeating the might of Hitler's U-boat fleet. Renowned regiments from the British Army came to garrison the town and famous men like Scott of the Antarctic, Gordon of Khartoum and boxer Jimmy Wilde were regular visitors.

These days, at first glance, the town seems to have only its history to recommend it. Yet this is far from the truth. A sense of history is all very well, indeed it is important, vitally important. We all need to know from where we have come. We need to have our origins and roots firmly embedded. But history is not an end in itself. Really, it is only the start.

To mis-quote the bard, Pembroke Dock has endured many 'slings and arrows of outrageous fortune'. As a community it has known the heights of elation and the depths of despair. The people of the town have endured or enjoyed it all with equanimity and good grace. Yes, they are aware of their glorious past but they also look to the future with hope. There are plans and there are schemes to develop the town, to bring back the prosperity that the place once knew. Some of these will fall by the wayside, just as many have fallen in the past, but some will succeed, some will achieve fruition. One thing is clear, the people of Pembroke Dock will never give up trying, will never sit back on their laurels, content with just their history to comfort and protect them.

The people of the town are a hardy breed – and that applies whether they are long time Pembroke Dock people or relative newcomers. The town has a very real ability to take people into its communal power. Very few people leave this place without it touching at least part of their heart and soul. A word of warning to anyone who might contemplate spending time in the town – once Pembroke Dock has touched you with its magic you will never be the same again.

And that is how it should be. Enjoy the sense of history that pervades every aspect of Pembroke Dock. Then look to the future with hope, enthusiasm and expectation.

Postscript

The land around Pembroke Dock was bought by the Admiralty when it first arrived, and the land under all the roads is still owned by the Ministry of Defence. With the navy came the post of Queen's Harbourmaster, responsible for the overseeing of shipping in the Pembroke Dock area. There has been a long-standing tradition of "beating the bounds" on the river between Pembroke Dock and Haverfordwest to mark the limits of the Queen's Harbourmaster's jurisdiction. A party of dignitaries, including the Mayor, sets off down river from Haverfordwest to meet the Queen's Harbourmaster on his boat. At their meeting point on the boundary between their two areas, they fire across each others' bows before sailing on for a celebratory drink together. The post of QHM has been part of the Royal Maritime Auxiliary Service who have been incumbents at the Mooring and Salvage depot for 30 years. Prior to that, the organisation the Port Auxiliary Service, which ran admiralty tugs, was based in Pembroke Dock and eventually became part of the Royal Maritime Auxiliary Service. They continued to employ hundreds of local people both in their offices and stores as well as on the tugs and ships.

It was the PAS who were also using the *Warrior* as a fuel jetty prior to its being taken to Portsmouth for restoration. The Royal Maritime Auxiliary Service is now being privatised and will be taken over by Serco Denholm, thereby cutting the final link between Pembroke Dock and the Navy. The post of the Queen's Harbourmaster, which is held by the senior officer at the base, will also end with Richard Craig, the current harbourmaster. The dockyard itself will become the property of The Milford Haven Port Authority.

Josephine Hammond
October 2006

Bibliography

Books

Anon, *The Guntower* (Pembs County Council, undated)

Carradice, Phil, *The Book of Pembroke Dock* (Barracuda Books, 1991)

——, *Welsh Shipwrecks in Camera* (Quotes, 1993)

——, *Wales at War* (Gomer, 2003)

Coles, John, *A Brief History of the Hospitals of Pembroke and Pembroke Dock* (Friends of South Pembs Hospital, undated)

Davies, W., Goddard, T., Scott, V., Evans, J., *PD Days* (Pembroke Dock Town Council, 1987)

Evans, John, *Flying Boat Haven* (Aviation and Maritime Research, 1985)

——, *Pembroke Dock Reflections* 2001 (Paterchurch Publications)

Davis, G. M., *The Loss of HMS Montagu* (privately printed, 1981)

Edwards, Sybil, *The Story of the Milford Haven Waterway* (Logaston Press, 2001)

David W. Howell (ed.), *Pembrokeshire County History, vol. iv* (Pembrokeshire Historical Society, 1993)

Findlay, James Anderson, *A Handbook of Pembroke Dock* (privately printed, 1875)

Hughes, Basil, *Jottings on the History of Pennar* (privately printed, 1991)

Johnson, Keith, *The Pubs of Pembroke, Pembroke Dock, Tenby and South Pembrokeshire* (Logaston Press, 2003)

Lloyd, T., Orbach, J., Scourfield, R., *The Buildings of Wales: Pembrokeshire* (Pevsner Guides, 2004)

MacDougall, Philip, *Royal Dockyards in Camera* (Quotes, 1989)

Mason, G., *Pembroke Dock* (1905)

Mayberry, Dr John, *I Saw Three Ships* (undated)

Miles, Dillwyn, *Megalithic Monuments* (Pembs Coast National Park, undated)

—— (ed.), *A Pembrokeshire Anthology* (Hughes & Son, 1983)

Peters, Mrs Stuart, *The History of Pembroke Dock* (Elliot Stock, 1905)

Reynolds, H. H. R., *Some Old Inns and Reminiscences of Pembroke Dock* (privately printed, 1939)

Richards, Bill, *Pembrokeshire Under Fire* (1965)

Scott, Vernon, *An Experience Shared* (Laleham Publications, 1992)

——, *Inferno 1940* (Western Telegraph, 1993)

——, *When the Poppies Bloom Again* (Pembs County Council, 1998)

Wheeler, N.J., *The Fortifications of Milford Haven and Pembroke Dock* (Pembs Coast National Park, undated)

Worsley, Roger, *The Pembrokeshire Explorer* (Coastal Cottages of Pembrokeshire, 1988)

Magazines/newspapers

Picture Postcard Monthly

The Western Telegraph

The West Wales Guardian

Sea Breezes

Welsh Rugby

Pembrokeshire Life

The Mariners Mirror

Primary sources

School Log Books, National School, Pembroke Dock

The *Blue Books*, 1847

'The 8th Royal Dockyard Battalion, Pembroke Dock' – original document held by Pembroke Dock Museum Trust

Pembroke Dock Centenary Programme of Celebration

Report on the State of Pembroke Dockyard, 1843 – original document held by Pembroke Dock Museum Trust

Interviews with John Walsh, Hubert Reynolds, Ted Owens, Bill Williams and Griffith John Jones

Acknowledgements

THANKS MUST GO to a wide variety of people and institutions: Firstly to Hazel Cushion and the staff of Accent Press for having the foresight and desire to see the history of Pembroke Dock told once more.

To John Evans of Paterchurch Publications, Vernon Scott and Lawrence Phillips for their research and scholarship over the years.

To Roy Hordley and Mrs D Waters via the John Evans Collection for the photographs of bomb damage during the Second World War. All other illustrations are from the author's own collection.

To those individuals who spoke to me about their experiences in the town during the war and in the years immediately afterwards, in particular John Walsh, Hubert 'Buzzer' Reynolds, Ted Owen, Griffith John Jones and Bill Williams.

To Ron Watts, curator of the Pembroke Dock Museum for his advice and help with sources and information.

To my family who, over the years, imbued me with a love of Pembroke Dock and its history, people like Arthur Morris and Ronnie and Fred Phillips who will never be forgotten in the town.

And last, but certainly not least, to my wife Trudy who, as always, has been unceasingly supportive and helpful with advice and – when needed – a damned good kick in the pants!

Index